Praise for *How to Remak Neighborhood by Neighborhood* . . .

"Our country is as divided today as it has been at any time since the Civil War and Reconstruction, not just in politics but in our society as well. Few have studied and thought more about how to bring a sense of community back to our local communities than Mack McCarter. He has developed a recipe for how to nourish and nurture the souls of our communities. Our neighborhoods, whether we realize it or not, are craving, even starving for something different, something to bring us together. This is a cookbook full of such recipes and thoughts."
—Charlie Cook, founder, The Cook Political Report

"My friend Mack, a true servant leader grounded in faith and hope, has written a book that is both compelling and necessary for our time and all time. From the moment of reading the introduction where tears flowed on my cheeks, to the last word, Mack has given us a path forward that may be new to some but is ancient in its wisdom."
—Matthew Dowd, political strategist, MSNBC analyst, and author, *A New Way: Embracing the Paradox as We Lead and Serve*

"Mack beautifully illustrates by words and actions what my homeless friend, Denver Moore, pounded into my brain. It is not the language we speak or the color of our skin that divides us, it's the condition of our hearts. This game changing book should be required reading for every person on the planet." **—Ron Hall, co-author of #1** *New York Times* **bestseller** *Same Kind of Different as Me*

"One of my all-time favorite movies is *Back to the Future*. Mack Mc-Carter doesn't have the wild hair of the scientist but 'by golly' he does have God's 'bolt of lightning' for plugging in best practices of his childhood into declining neighborhoods. Here he shares the courageous steps he took to fuse love and caring into relationships using best elements of society to improve neighborhoods, cities and our futures." **—Linda C. Fuller, co-founder of Habitat for Humanity International and The Fuller Center for Housing**

"The practical guidance in this volume for bringing about fundamental change in our communities draws on insights about humanity flowing from Aristotle through Weber to behavioral economics. It also subtly recounts one man's journey of discerning a true vocation. Wonderfully written, it is truly inspirational."—**Christopher L. Holoman, PhD president, Centenary College of Louisiana**

"Mack McCarter, by caring for others on a massive scale has truly made the world a better place. This book tells how he did it."—**Bennett Johnston, four-term U.S. Senator from Louisiana**

"If you have any concern for the future of our nation, or if you are lacking in hope, I ask you to give this book the serious attention it deserves."—**Frank F. Islam, entrepreneur and author,** *Renewing the American Dream* **and** *Working the Pivot Points*

"A must read! Mack McCarter is a truly remarkable man who daily lives the commandment to love his neighbor as himself. Mack has laid out the blueprint for changing our world into loving, connected communities."—**John H. Dalton, chair of the national advisory board of Community Renewal and 70th Secretary of the Navy**

"Mack McCarter has spent a lifetime forging loving communities out of complete strangers. This revealing and thoughtful book documents how caring, friendship, and the gift of kindness can bring about powerful changes in our world. It sounds so simple, and that's his point. He reminds us that loving each other isn't hard to do, it just takes practice."—**Lee Cowan, correspondent,** *CBS Sunday Morning*

"Mack McCarter has found the best formula for repairing a broken world—and describes it in this book. The formula is so simple, which is why it is so effective and why I was eager to jump at the opportunity to support it in our company's 'neighborhood.' Just imagine how much better the world would be if everyone followed Mack's passion to bring love, kindness and caring to one person, one city block, or neighborhood."—**Patrick Ottensmeyer, CEO, Kansas City Southern Railway Company**

How to Remake the World
Neighborhood by Neighborhood

How to Remake the World Neighborhood by Neighborhood

Mack McCarter

Founder, Community Renewal International

with Tim Muldoon

ORBIS BOOKS

Maryknoll, New York 10545

Manufactured in the United States of America.
Manuscript editing and typesetting by Joan Weber Laflamme.

Library of Congress Cataloging-in-Publication Data

Names: McCarter, Mack, 1945– author. | Muldoon, Tim, author.
Title: How to remake the world neighborhood by neighborhood / Mack McCarter, Founder, Community Renewal International with Tim Muldoon.
Description: Maryknoll, New York : Orbis Books, [2022] | Includes bibliographical references. | Summary: "A model of community renewal is spreading around the world, attracting supporters ready to serve others"— Provided by publisher.
Identifiers: LCCN 2022015610 | ISBN 9781626985001 (trade paperback) | ISBN 9781608339624 (epub)
Subjects: LCSH: Church and the world. | Change—Religious aspects—Christianity. | Neighborhoods.
Classification: LCC BR115.W6 M365 2022 | DDC 261—dc23 eng/20220601
LC record available at https://lccn.loc.gov/2022015610

To my wife, Judy, whose quiet love of God and steadfast treasuring of every person powerfully strengthens the two of us to step out through Hope's Door and march off the map each day, walking by the Faith that Love does work, and that Love will win.

—*Mack*

Contents

**Part Three
Grounding in Friendship**

Foreword

by Donnie Simpson

I met Mack McCarter through my daughter, Dawn. She and her boyfriend, John, called him Uncle Mack and then "Marrying Mack," as he was the one who officiated their wedding a few years later. She had told me that he reminded her so much of me and that we were the same kind of people. I have to tell you that upon first seeing him, I couldn't understand why.

We were clearly from different sides of the track. He would quote Matthew and Socrates and I'd quote Stevie and Marley. He used phrases like "By golly!" and let's just say I didn't. He asked me to come down to Shreveport to host the twentieth anniversary celebration of Community Renewal International (CRI). I agreed, and I'm so glad I did. Not only did I get to meet one of my idols, President Jimmy Carter, but I got to meet so many people from so many walks of life who were just as dedicated as Mack and the president to making our communities better.

Mack told me how, more than thirty years ago, he started knocking on doors in neighborhoods that were rife with prostitution, drugs, and gangs. He was rejected at first, but after

---

Donnie Simpson is host of the *Donnie Simpson Show* on WMMJ-FM in Washington, DC, and a class of 2020 inductee into the Radio Hall of Fame.

several Saturday mornings of persistent knocks, he was on the couch in conversations about how, together, we can transform this community.

Police statistics show the undeniable impact CRI had in these communities. Crime dropped more than 50 percent, and people were back on their front porches again, free of the fear that had imprisoned them for so many years.

On a personal note, Mack has changed my life. I honestly believe that there's no way you can meet Mack McCarter and not be changed. His heart is so pure. There's something about him that makes you want to be better. At the risk of sounding blasphemous, I feel like being Mack's friend is like having Jesus on speed dial.

The streets of Shreveport and Bossier City didn't know what they were up against. You may be tough, but look closely at the belt buckles of these love warriors. That double G isn't for Gucci, it's for God's Gang and there ain't no stopping them. The thing about Mack and CRI, though, is that they weren't looking to exclude anyone. They were looking to include them and repurpose their attributes to help remake the world.

While Mack can quote some of the greatest philosophers of all time, I'd like to share a quotation from Earth, Wind & Fire. In "All About Love," frontman Maurice White sings, "You gotta love you. And learn all the beautiful things around you. . . . And if there ain't no beauty, you got to make some beauty. Have mercy!"

Mack McCarter is all about love. And if seeing people, seeing value in them, and loving them is the common trait that my daughter saw in me and Mack, then "by golly," she was right.

PART ONE

SEEING THE NEED

Introduction

We Can Grow a More Caring World

His name is Thomas H. Thigpen and I saw him fly. I am sure I did.

Thomas H. Thigpen and I shared two things in common. We were born in the vintage years of the 1940s in Shreveport, Louisiana. And we grew up on the easy side of town. The South has its own bitter version of apartheid, its tribal separation a lifestyle, and we happened to be born into the more privileged tribe. Tommy's prominent family propelled him into a successful career within Shreveport's inner circle of business winners. I left the city to pastor cowboys in West Texas.

In the twenty-five-year interim, living in a place distant from the business and politics of my hometown, I had forgotten all about Thigpen. After all, he was younger by two years and had been barely noticeable to the older high-school crowd. Then I came home to Shreveport finally prepared for my life's work— that of serving a city of everybody, a city I had long loved.

By mobilizing other "bridge people" all over the city for four years, quietly building foundations of loving relationships across all the variables of human diversity, and then systematically following a simple but comprehensive strategy to restore community to a city about to bust, I was unknowingly put on a collision course with Thomas H. Thigpen.

Of course, word had gotten out about me and about "us," the folks reaching out to one and all through Shreveport's Community Renewal. Only four months after returning to my hometown in 1991, I was visiting one of the Black congregations that anchors the entire region, the Mount Canaan Missionary Baptist Church. I had heard of the pastor, the Reverend Doctor Harry Blake. I had read of his close association with Martin Luther King Jr. during the civil rights era, but there was so much I did not know. I was only visiting to build bridges, a kind of perfunctory ambassadorial tip-of-the-hat. Little did I know what deep water I was about to enter! Wholly unplanned and wholly unreasonably, I, the white visitor, was led to join Mount Canaan that day. (This is another story in itself, which continues to unfold in relational richness up to this very moment.) The word spread.

Not long thereafter, the news of my spending time in a prominent Black church in town reached a friend of Tommy's. This friend called me. He told me that he had a friend who was consumed by the gall of racial hatred. Would I call his friend and have lunch with him? He was talking about Tommy. He told me that Tommy Thigpen thought he remembered me as the guy whose football career ended with a leg bone splitting to the knee. He was right. I phoned Tommy for lunch, and we agreed to meet the next day.

On Wednesday, January 18, high noon, we took a table at the Madison Square Garden. No sooner were we seated when the dam burst and Tommy spewed, "I hate ———s!" (Everyone knows the slur that dripped acidly from his lips.) "Now what are you gonna do about it? 'Cause I believe they are ruining everything, and I moved to the lake to get away. And one other thing you need to know. . . . Two days ago I pulled a gun out of my glove compartment and leveled it at two of 'em, and I'm scared of what I almost did. So what are you gonna do, because something radical has got to be done!"

Honestly. I just sat there, but my mind was racing like a blender. I was on overload and almost panicked for lack of an answer. Here, sitting across from me in a booth, was a guy who quite simply personified one of the most monstrous evils pressing against the fragile dike of today's America. I was blank. Then, by the grace of God, I heard words coming out of my mouth.

"Tommy, tonight is our prayer meeting at Mount Canaan. I want you to go with me."

Thigpen jerked straight backward as though a steel rod had been shoved up his spine. He was quiet. Then he snake-slitted his eyes and said, "All right, I'll go." It was more of a challenge than an acceptance.

So I pushed: "And one other thing, I don't want you telling anyone that you are going to Mount Canaan before we go. You can tell 'em tomorrow, but not before we go. Agreed?"

A smart, "Why?" shot back at me.

"Because, I don't want you to tease about going to a Black church with your friends. If you really want some answers, then you will agree."

And like a man who believes he is holding five aces, Tommy agreed.

"Good, I'll pick you up at six-thirty."

Thigpen got into the car that evening, and he was quiet. When we turned at the downtown light that leads into Allendale, the Black neighborhood where the church is located, I said, "Now, Tommy, you are gonna see me hug the men at Mount Canaan, and you will see me kiss the cheeks of the ladies. So don't look shocked. And just remember that you are a guest, because that is how we do." He simply nodded.

I walked into the foyer of the church, with a dead man walking a step behind me. I was grabbed and hugged by the men and kissed by the ladies. Love rules there. And in their innocence, so often injured, they mistook Tommy for a friend because he was with their friend Mack. So they hugged him and kissed him too. We hug our family. We hug our friends. (They simply assumed that a racist would never come to their prayer meeting, because forever they have watched the racists go to their own church meetings.)

We finally sat down in the pew. Tommy sat stiff, his arms crossed over his chest. Then we began to chant one of the long-metered songs that open the service. If you close your eyes, that pre-freedom old chant would take you to a brush arbor in the company of those who had "stealed away to Jesus" more than a century ago. I wondered what Thomas H. Thigpen was thinking. I dared not turn to look. But I cut my eyes his way while still facing straight ahead. And out of the corner of my eye, all I could see was his elbow, folded chest high resting across his heart, and it was shaking like crazy! Was he laughing?

I whipped around to sting him, but I never got the chance. Tears were streaming under his glasses and dripping off his cheeks. The silent sobbing was shaking his whole body, elbows and all. He whispered because he couldn't speak. He breathed, "I feel like I've come home." And I knew he meant it.

That evening, Sister Sharon Lattier brought the meditation message. She spoke of the hurt and the rejection and the soul pain that she feels every single day because of the color of her skin in Shreveport, Louisiana. Then, from experienced eloquence in expressive "love living," she told of the freedom that is hers when her spirit soars in forgiving the littleness of small hearts. The Unseen Heart of All Love could not have used a more devastatingly effective scalpel in lancing the boil of hate within Thomas H. Thigpen than the sweetness of that Love mediated through Sharon's whole being. He was absolutely ruined.

Tommy cried all the way through the whole prayer meeting. And as we closed our time together, at the end of the meeting, Pastor Blake, by custom, said, "Mack, I see that you have a guest. Would you stand and introduce him?" Tommy and I stood up together. "Pastor and church, this is Tommy Thigpen, an old friend from high school." The irrepressible Blake laughed, "Thigpen! Why every Thigpen I know is filthy rich! Would you like to give expressions, Mr. Thigpen?" Tommy looked blankly at me. "What does he mean?" "Tommy, he wants you to say something." I saw Thigpen grab the back of the pew in front of us with both hands to steady himself. And I sat down.

Then, Thomas H. Thigpen, white, rich, businessman tribe, spoke: "I came here tonight with hate in my heart. But you have loved me out of that hate, and I feel like I've come home for the first time in my life." And with those expressions, Tommy lowered his head and began to cry.

We were all simply stunned. We couldn't move.

But not Pastor Blake! He flew with the flash of an angel. Down the aisle. Into our pew he flew before reaching out with strong arms and clutching my new and old friend to himself and just holding him and holding him. Tommy put his head on Pastor Blake's chest and sobbed and sobbed and sobbed. I was crying too. I just couldn't help it. Blake was crying. Our whole church cried. That healing hug must have lasted at least three full minutes. Then they gently broke and Pastor Blake started back to the altar.

But Tommy shot out of the pew after him, caught him half-way down the aisle, and almost desperately—like a drowning man clutching a lifeline—sobbed again like a baby. It was then that the church started shouting.

Now you need to know about the Reverend Doctor Harry Blake. He was reared on a plantation north of Shreveport, the son of a sharecropper trapped by the company store all of his life. When Pastor Blake was twenty-five years old, he was the president of the then-outlawed NAACP in Shreveport. It was 1963, and that was when the monsters bombed the Sixteenth Street Baptist Church in Birmingham, Alabama, and killed those four precious little girls all dressed up in their Sunday best: Denise McNair, Cynthia Wesley, Carole Robertson, and Addie Mae Collins. And Harry Blake called for a memorial service for them to be held here in Shreveport at the Little Union Baptist Church.

The politicians were usually no help. There was Bull Conner, the white supremacist Birmingham Commissioner of Public Safety who had fire hoses and attack dogs set upon civil rights activists in his town, and in Shreveport at that time we had the miserable George D'Artois. He told Blake that there would be no meeting. But Harry Blake went ahead anyway. D'Artois and over two hundred policemen surrounded the church that afternoon. They demanded that the mourners exit two by two and do so immediately. Then they went in and dragged Pastor Blake outside and with their nightsticks and billy clubs beat him almost to death.

Isaiah prophesies that "the wolf and the lamb shall lie down together." Well, I figure that this asks the wolf only to change its appetite. But it asks everything of the lamb! My race and Tommy's race has been the wolf to Pastor Blake's race. And here Blake came down the aisle to hug and embrace a man who had hated him without knowing him. Now isn't that something? You and I know that it is!

Yes. I saw a man fly with angel's wings that night. I am sure that I did.

It sure was true for Tommy. That night I thought that I would never get Thigpen out of the church to go home. Tommy was hugging and kissing everyone in sight. When we finally got into the car, Tommy positively glowed. "I'm free!" he cried. Then he said it again as if he were tasting it. "I'm free. I feel filled up with love!"

Thigpen began to show up every Wednesday night for prayer meeting. If someone got up during "prayer needs" time to tell of their needs, I would see Tommy with them after the services, likely as not with his arm around them, speaking quiet words of consolation. Tommy's wife, Frances, started coming too. In fact, Tommy even brought Ron Mercer, the friend who called me in the first place. They all said, "This is the place where love lives, and where love is, God is."

Tommy soon joined the Mount Canaan Missionary Baptist Church. He became the third white person in a congregation of over two thousand members. In December, Tommy was asked to be the co-chairman of the Men's Day Annual Celebration at Mount Canaan. He called me immediately to tell of the honor. He was as thrilled as a child.

A year later, Thomas H. Thigpen called me for lunch. It was one year to the day that we had eaten together. We went back to the Madison Square Garden. When we sat down, Tommy said, "Do you remember the first words I said to you a year ago?"

"I sure do, Tommy. I don't think I'll ever forget them. You talked about hating a group of people."

"That's right, Mack," said Tommy. "Do you remember the second thing I said?"

No, I couldn't remember.

Tommy leaned across the table and said, "I added that they've made a terrible mess and something radical has got to be done about it." Tommy leaned back and with a delicious blend of irony and wonder said something I will never forget. He said, "You know when I said that, I had no idea that the radical solution to this situation was the radical transformation of this self."

A hug and an embrace. While we hug those who are close, we must embrace all. And we can never truly embrace all unless we hug those who are close. Pastor Blake's courageous embrace was a healing hug for Tommy! And Tommy's willing hug led to a healing embrace of all. Because Pastor Blake flew to Tommy, Tommy now flies.

I've seen many souls afflicted with the "narrows" and the "limits" and the "littles" when it comes to others. I've seen them become whole and large in life and soul. I am sure that you have too. But if you think for one moment that folks can't fly, then come see me. I will take you to see Thomas H. Thigpen. I tell you, I saw him fly! I have never been more certain of anything in my life.

Our organization, Community Renewal International, is deeply involved in helping peculiarly sick people to get well. In what follows, I share with you how we are building the foundations of an ever-caring world and multiplying stories like Tommy's.

1

We Can Remake Our Communities

The fundamental challenge facing humankind is the repetitive failure of our societies to create and grow a total community that incrementally and generationally improves the flourishing of all its members. We have never created a society that is ever renewing itself infinitely. We have never made a society that simply gets better and better and better with limitless possibilities of human development. Not only is this true globally, but the history of our human race shows that every major society has gone through continuous cycles of growth and decline and even death. Lurching toward some dream and hope for human betterment only to falter and ultimately fail seems our historical lot.

We are living at a time when our interconnectivity is suddenly more than the incisive imaginings of our prophets and poets. Our entire global family is now binding together in every way possible. What affects one affects all. I did not think at one time that the United States was inextricably connected to what went on in Afghanistan. Indeed, at one time it wasn't. But then September 11, 2001, came. In that nightmare I realized that what happens in Afghanistan and all over the world can and does affect all of us.

Early in the days of the COVID-19 pandemic I was reminded of this insight. Never before had I given thought to the economic niceties of production and supply chains in places like

China, India, or the Philippines, but as the shelves of my local grocery store ran thin I recalled how irreversibly our world has become interdependent. "No man is an island, entire of itself," wrote the English poet John Donne in the sixteenth century, and his words are even truer today.

So the challenge that is now starkly before us, is this: we must come together in such a way that we can create a global society that has learned in its maturity to actually grow better and better human beings contributing to a whole community that is ever improving in all things that touch upon our lives here on planet earth. Because only by acting together as an entire global family in a consciously cooperative way can we possibly have even the remotest chance of securing the health of our planet. There is no Planet B.

I have devoted my life to finding our way forward in answering this fundamental challenge facing humankind: creating a global society that grows better and better with no stop sign in its future. How in the world can we do that? How can we, of all people, accomplish something that has never been done in our entire history? Indeed, Lewis Mumford, the great seer of human society, lamented the chief enigma of history: why do we keep collapsing the societies we construct?[1] So is it possible? Can we do it?

Over the past three decades I've become convinced that the answer is through *connecting caring people*. My home town of Shreveport, Louisiana, is proof that caring for each and all works, because it responds to the most fundamental longings of the human heart. In these pages I share the story of how connecting people who care for one another has transformed entire neighborhoods of the city, giving people hope and helping to rebuild lives. Rich and poor; Black, white, and brown;

---

[1] American sociologist, historian, and philosopher of technology. See Lewis Mumford, *The Transformations of Man* (London: Allen and Unwin, 1957).

Democrat and Republican; old and young—over fifty thousand of my neighbors have joined our movement, and block by block, neighborhood by neighborhood, we are remaking the world. Our poorest, formerly most crime-ridden neighborhoods have seen crime rates cut in half, and families are once again able to walk outside and get to know their neighbors. Home ownership and high school graduation rates have risen. Our neighborhoods are places where neighbors know one another and regularly work together to build community across socioeconomic and racial lines. Thousands of volunteers across the region regularly dedicate tens of thousands of hours to provide educational and social support to children and teens, even from the lowest income brackets; adults have opportunities to earn their high school diplomas; networks of neighbors provide leads for jobs and economic opportunity. The evidence has been confirmed by our local police departments and governments—Shreveport and our neighbors in Bossier City (it's pronounced BO-zhur) are building a society in which all people can thrive.

This is the story of how we built a movement that has now been replicated in cities and towns around the country, and even halfway around the world. As I write, friends in places like Shawnee, Oklahoma; Abilene, Texas; and now Washington, DC, are working together to rebuild the relational foundations of their communities so that they too might grow and flourish. Villages in Cameroon and Nigeria are beginning the process of community renewal too, after seeing firsthand what is happening in Shreveport-Bossier. There are schools here in Louisiana that are building their curriculum on our model, and already this same model is providing a map of how to build community on university campuses. We are working with a major healthcare system to expand its public-health outreach in the community, and we are breaking ground on an exciting new initiative with a corporate partner with deep roots in our city.

Not long ago *CBS Sunday Morning* featured our organization, Community Renewal International, in a piece that highlighted our dreams for how to remake the world. In my interview I reflected on a memory from my childhood in the late 1940s and early 1950s: how the fear of polio seized so many families and made them afraid to engage in ordinary activities, like going to a swimming pool on a hot summer's day. I recalled how the work of Dr. Jonas Salk rid us of the scourge of polio and changed people's lives on a wide scale. So much so, I said, that my granddaughter once asked me "PaPa, what is polio?" How could something so fearsome, I thought, become completely forgotten just two generations later?

My hope today is that one day children will ask their grandparents a question similar to the one my granddaughter asked me. They will ask, "PaPa, what is hate?"

Back to Beginnings

About twice a week I walk down the street where I was born and where I grew up and lived until I married at the ripe old age of twenty-two. It wasn't a rich neighborhood but it was a great street. We were all wealthy beyond our dreams. And each time that I walk down my old street and pass the corner house on the south side at 271 East Fairview, a flood of memories rushes through my mind and suddenly I am home again.

It is summer, and we are busy building tree houses, digging forts, and having dirt clod battles with other streets to see who can claim Querbes Park. No doors were locked. Evenings saw all the neighbors sitting on the porch after supper where the front yards were transformed into our dens and we played group games until we couldn't make each other out even with the porch lights on. I remember when our street was paved and we got sidewalks. There were bicycle races and chases galore. And every summer we put on a group talent show and charged a dollar each to our parents to watch us sing, dance, recite poems, and generally just cut up.

All the moms watched all the kids on the street and, of course, had spanking privileges with every child! Who ever heard of a home burglar alarm in the late 1940s and 1950s when I grew up on East Fairview? I walk down that street today and I can tell you where everyone lived. I think of all the kids and wonder where the East Fairview urban diaspora has taken us.

It was all so typical. And that is precisely the point. Because it no longer is. Our world has changed. The streets we grew up on have been transformed into a twenty-first-century model of "neighborhood lite." Very little interaction with our neighbors is the hallmark of today. We can email friends all over the world, but we rarely know who is living and perhaps dying only five houses down the block. We have become gradually disconnected from our neighbors while becoming virtually connected worldwide.

This disconnection with our next-door neighbors, our street village, is symptomatic of societal disintegration. So I walk down my old street twice a week to remind me that we must return to the basics.

My memories reinforce my calling. I have learned that caring alone cannot stop the collapse of community, but caring together can. I have learned that only by connecting and reconnecting caring people can we reweave the fundamental fabric of human society so necessary for our children and their children to thrive. And walking down my old street redirects me to a single-minded mission in the midst of what appears to be such a complex and plural world where busyness is ever distracting from life.

How do we put it all back together? I remember that the great man of letters, and toast of all of eighteenth-century England, Dr. Samuel Johnson, was told as a boy by his cousin Cornelius Ford that great minds make the mistake of studying the intricacies of the leaves and the limbs of the tree. Ford told him that he must learn to "grasp the trunk hard only, and you will shake all the branches."[2] So the answer in rebuilding and restoring the neighborhoods that can nurture and nourish quality living is to invest ourselves in a *simple, systematic,* and *intentional* process of connecting caring people where they live. This model can then be replicated over and over until a city is leavened. That city then becomes a model for other cities until a nation is leavened.[3]

It takes a dedicated group of people to be full-time community nurturers. They must learn how to motivate and mobilize and train others, while nourishing the relationships of friendships that are forming and teaching them to become nurturers themselves. Then we will have thousands who will walk down their old streets and remember and respond to the call of those memories. You too can glimpse a new future when you commit yourself to be a neighbor.

This is our mission here. We call it community renewal. And our one sentence synopsis is also our bugle call, "Community Renewal International has developed a model which concretely *initiates*, systematically *generates*, and methodically *sustains* safe and caring human society with real, measurable, and remarkable results!" Together we can go back home. Together we must!

----

[2] W. Jackson Bate, *Samuel Johnson* (New York: Harcourt Brace Jovanovich, 1977), 51.

[3] The image of leaven—yeast that makes bread rise—comes from the Gospels (Mt 13:33; Lk 13:20–21). This image suggests that a small group of people function the way that a small amount of yeast functions in making bread rise; they can transform an entire society by providing the conditions that lift people and communities so that they thrive.

What Is a Society?

Many of us are able to pinpoint the vital days of our lives. And that we cannot predict the future with certainty as we travel on this journey of life, we are able to look back and to see the critical turns and the salient choices which determined the adventure itself. We know the turning points as we reflect. We can discern those decisions, for good or for ill, that launched our steps and thus molded our character and fixed our destiny. It is not unusual for each of us to have at least a handful of those days.

One of those days came for me in the week following Easter Sunday in 1977. My mother had invited Dr. D. Elton Trueblood to come to Shreveport, speak for the week at the Kings Highway Christian Church, and stay in our home. He accepted! I was flabbergasted. You see, Dr. Trueblood, to those of my generation and the generation before us, was a true titan. He had written nearly forty books and the words and work of this great Quaker philosopher and theologian were soaked up by thousands of us. He was one of my heroes, and he was staying in my home in Shreveport! I could not believe it.

I was the pastor of a congregation in West Texas at the time and a wet behind the ears thirty-two year old. I preached the shortest Easter sermon in recorded history and caught a flight to Shreveport to spend the week with Dr. Trueblood. I got in late that night. Dr. Trueblood had already retired. All I could think about was simply talking with him. Could I speak without my voice shaking? Would I betray myself with idiocy as I had done a thousand times before? Could I say one thing, anything, intelligent? So my sleep that night was a restless, anticipatory repose.

The next morning I could hear Dr. Trueblood's deeply resonant seventy-seven-year-old voice holding forth to a small group of folks gathered in our downstairs den. I showered and dressed as quickly as I could and literally bounded down the stairs, turned the corner, and after introductions, sat down with a truly great man. That was forty-five years ago. And it seems like yesterday.

Within one minute of my taking a seat, Dr. Trueblood (how can I ever forget this!) said: "The American congregations are doing many good things, but they are not stopping the disintegration of our society. And we must find an effective means to arrest this collapse and to reconstruct the foundations which can renew our communities!" That was it. Those two sentences, uttered with decades of deep conviction from the man whose voice had cried out for awakening and renewal in our country and its churches, stopped me dead in my tracks and spun me around to face a new road now rising before me.

Of course, my first few steps were those of a toddler unable to grasp the wide horizons of new worlds yet unseen. I spoke, "Yes, Dr. Trueblood, we do live in a sick society." That was it. That was the best I could do. I was just thankful that my voice hadn't cracked. Then he leaned forward, and said, "Young man, what do you mean by . . . " and I thought he was going to say, "by sick?" And I was ready with the recitation of societal pathology. But no! Dr. Trueblood said, "Young man, what do you mean by society?" I was as blank as a goose. Dr. Trueblood knew that if we couldn't define it, we could not heal it. And so my journey began.

Healing Relationships: Learning from History

So how do we take what seems like this jumbled mass of self-willed creatures we call human beings and find a unifying principle that we can apply in practical ways to create a community that is ever renewing us, our conditions, and our world?

The answer came for me in a very simple way. I was reading a book that Dr. Trueblood said I must read. But it wasn't just a book. It was the third volume of the twelve-volume work by Arnold J. Toynbee called *A Study of History*. This project took Toynbee twenty-seven years to complete. His idea was to give a broad-brush approach to the panorama of the various civilizations that have marched across our globe, and to compare and contrast them. It is a fascinating work, which I heartily commend. (According to an editor of his work, Toynbee suggested that "a society does not ever die 'from natural causes,' but always dies from suicide or murder—and nearly always from the former.")[4]

But what totally arrested me, what sat me straight up in my chair, was Toynbee's definition of society. When I read his definition, I distinctly declared, "If that is true—if indeed it is true—then, not only can we stop the repetitive cycle of declining civilizations, but we can actually grow societies that can get better and better and better." Here is what Toynbee wrote that set me off like a skyrocket: Society is a system of relationships.[5]

I now know that that statement and that insight are at the very heart of the nature of our social life, and are totally true. But when I read that statement on October 27, 1981, I only understood the second part of his encompassing observation. I knew about relationships. At the time, I was thirty-six years old and had pastored churches for ten years. I certainly did not claim to know everything. But I did know that a pastor is at best

---

[4] D. C. Somervell, describing Toynbee's work on the breakdown of civilizations, in Arnold Toynbee, *A Study of History: Abridgement of Volumes I–VI*, ed. D. C. Somervell and David Churchill Somervell (New York: Oxford University Press, 1957), 318.

[5] "The truth seems to be that a human society is, in itself a relation: a particular kind of relation between human beings who are not only individuals but are also social animals in the sense that they could not exist at all . . . without being in this social relation with one another." "A society, we may say, is a relation beween individual." Toynbee, *A Study of History,* vol. III (New York: Oxford University Press, 1934), 223, 230.

a physician of relationships. And I knew that relationships had rules, and that those rules were just as strong and real as the laws of gravity. As I meditated on this idea that society is a system of relationships, it gradually became clear that the phrase was missing one word: *positive*. Society, I now am utterly convinced, is a system of *positive* relationships.

The Streets of Shreveport

I was eager to bring this insight about society to my congregation. Surely, I thought, the church community would understand that it was called by God to develop and sustain the relational foundation of society. We formed and launched the Cornerstone Christian Community Movement to invite people to reflect on their call to love God and neighbor, and like the early monastic communities commit themselves to preserving and then rebuilding society.

In retrospect, I see how much I missed the mark in my early efforts to develop the model. I still believe that churches can be important places to nurture in people a desire to heal the world by committing themselves to care for others, but I underestimated how entrenched people's attitudes can be. Many who were part of the church had not signed up to be catalysts for renewal and did not see their discipleship as involving the kind of commitment that renewal of society called for. Church for too many people was a place of refuge from society rather than an incubator of an emerging, transformed society.

So in 1991 I resigned as pastor and moved with my family back to my hometown. I had kept my dear friend Milton Hamel, whom I'd known since the age of four, aware of the kind of work I was doing and my plans for community renewal. Milton invited me to return and made it possible for me to devote myself to building the model.

Milton was a successful businessman in Shreveport, and he had witnessed the decline of the city in the wake of the economic changes in the 1980s. The city had lost some sixty thousand citizens during those years as industries left and businesses closed. Milton had little time for piety, but he was deeply interested in the basic idea that it was possible to rebuild the relational foundation of communities, and so begin the restoration of society. Decline, poverty, violence—these signs of a sick society—he understood, were also bad for business. That insight stays with me to this day as we build connections to the world of business, which I'll describe later.

So putting his trust in me, Milton opened doors to the world of business throughout Shreveport. He was later part of the original board of the newly formed Shreveport Community Renewal (later Shreveport-Bossier Community Renewal) and helped make possible the early funding that businesses contributed in the hope of stemming the tide of decline.

Armed with the conviction that Toynbee had it right in assessing the nature of society as a system of relationships (remember to add "positive" to qualify "relationships"), and hoping that love was the crucial ingredient in that formula, I determined to see if it really worked. I knew that it was one thing to preach love inside the walls to a congregation of likeminded folks, but I didn't know if it really worked to power up a renewing of our whole city and a whole society. I was shocked to discover that the city I had left in the bloom of youth in 1963 was a different place when I returned. In the midst of wonderfully hopeful developments, like the end of racial segregation and separation of the races, there was now the awful prevalence of crime fueled by drugs that had simply not been a part of my existence growing up in Shreveport in the decades of the forties, fifties, and sixties. Now, gangs, drive-by shootings, a skyrocketing murder rate, and an oil-based economy "in the tank" seemed to be sinking the city. People were leaving in droves. I was shocked. Could love really do the job?

I was determined to find out. I struck out to find an effective way to be an instrument of what I had preached about all of those years. Only two months after arriving on the scene, I heard of a group of people who were going each week into the most forlorn neighborhood, Allendale, and seeking to become friends with the folks who lived there in what they called "the Bottoms." At the time, the neighborhood averaged two homicides per week.

Allendale was not always this way. Once upon a time this neighborhood had boasted large Victorian houses and was home to the white citizens who wanted access to farmland and horse pastures. As those residents moved out of the city, Allendale became a rental hub for the largely African American population of laborers: farmhands, domestics, and other blue-collar workers. By 1920, this neighborhood, named after Confederate general and later governor Henry Watkins Allen, had become almost entirely African American. And it thrived.

Shreveport in the early twentieth century was not well disposed to be a model of racial harmony. Caddo Parish, where Allendale is located, was the last place on land where the Confederate flag had been lowered after the Civil War, and in 1906 a Confederate monument bearing the likeness of Allen and other generals was dedicated at the parish courthouse. That monument remained until the tense summer of 2020 and the protests that followed the killing of George Floyd.

The move of African Americans into Allendale had begun in the 1880s, and within a few decades they had developed a vibrant community that included churches, businesses, entertainment venues, and many residences. The Bottoms was added to the National Register of Historic Places in 1984 in large part because of this thriving culture, where in its heyday in the 1940s you could patronize Black businesses by day and take in a show by the likes of Louis Armstrong or Cab Calloway by night.

But the problems that afflicted many US cities starting in the 1970s did not spare Allendale. The houses that had been built decades earlier had fallen into disrepair, and many residents began leaving, so that by 1990 the population had been cut in half. Gangs and drugs moved in during the 1980s, a period that also saw the federal government intervene in Shreveport's stagnant efforts to desegregate schools. Allendale had become a shell of its former self; rather than a tight-knit, self-sustaining community, it was a segregated community in decline.

I had participated in the civil rights movement and had a commitment to growing in relationship with members of the Black community. So I joined with others walking through Allendale, and was assigned one of the most dangerous streets. The day came when I got in my car and drove down to Lawrence Street. It was a street not far from downtown, and it was lined with houses that in the South we call shotgun houses—small homes with rooms laid out in a straight line. When I was growing up many of our Black folks had to endure those houses, of which few had indoor plumbing. I determined to go.

I met with the people who were scattering into the neighborhood and then I went to my street. It was about ten o'clock on a Saturday morning, so I figured that all of the "bad guys" would have a hangover from the night before and it would be a little safer. But still I thought, "I am going to die." This was not unreasonable. There were some powerful obstacles operating against me. And I knew that I was just not the strongest ambassador for the love that we had. I was still real shaky.

Here I was going to meet strangers.

I was a different skin color.

I lived on a different economic level.

And because of the prevalence of violent crime, I was flat-out scared.

Those are some pretty massive mountains to move. I drove to the street and the overwhelming urge to keep driving seized me. I told myself, *I'll just do a drive-by blessing! "Bless you. Bless you. Bless you all,"* as I roar on through. But I was compelled to stop and park.

Thank goodness I did. It changed my life. I slowly got out of the car, and when I did, a whole group of children came running up to me to greet me. I picked up one in each arm and I had a child hanging on my back (this is true! I also admit that the thought ran through my head, "they won't shoot their own kids!") and I walked up the steps to that first shotgun house and knocked on the door. It opened a bit and I blurted, "I'm Mack McCarter and there is a whole group of us who believe that if we can get to be friends then we can change this city."

Not many doors opened. But now emboldened, I went back every Saturday morning at ten o'clock in the morning. I went with nothing but me. I offered only friendship. And within three months, at ten each Saturday morning, I would find the folks on Lawrence Street sitting on the front porches of those shotgun houses waiting for their friend to come and sit up with them and talk with them, shooting the breeze, as we used to call it.

The Power of Friendship

One of the many stories that unfolded during that period was with a man I'll call Isaiah, a well-known drug dealer. He had turned to this work because there were no other opportunities for him, and he needed to feed his partner and their four children. They were doing their best, and Isaiah himself was just trying to be a good father. Everyone in the neighborhood knew this—

there was no sense of outrage or disdain for him, because all of them had similarly experienced the lack of opportunities open to Black citizens at the time. People knew he was a drug dealer, but by golly (they said) he's our drug dealer. He's our neighbor.

Isaiah and I got to be friends. One evening I was out on Fannin Street, which was known to be the worst street in Shreveport. It was home to the Bottoms Boys, a notorious gang known to sometimes shoot at cars passing by. I was with a group from a local congregation, and we were singing together. We stood opposite a fairly large house with a long porch, and eventually I saw Isaiah passing by. I shouted a hello to him and walked toward him. He smiled, but then the smile faded. Then he did something astonishing.

Isaiah walked up onto the porch, then to the edge, and jumped over the railing. He ran toward me in the middle of the street I was crossing to greet him, and grabbed me in a big bear hug. As he kept his body between me and the house, he walked me backward across the street. I thought, *Man, he is really glad to see me!*

I later learned that the house was the headquarters of the Bottoms Boys, and that he was on his way in to get his weekly supplies. Already members of the gang had their guns trained on me as I was walking across the street toward the house. They were ready to shoot, had Isaiah not kept himself in their line of fire. It was the most powerful example of the power of loving friendship that I had ever experienced.

Over time, Isaiah's life changed. He eventually left the drug trade and devoted his life to God. He now has full-time employment in a local business due to friendships that he developed through our network. To this day Isaiah plays drums in a church. His life has been transformed, as have the lives of his wife and children.

Ezekiel, the ancient prophet appointed by God to speak to his people in exile in Babylon, writes about going to sit with the exiles:

> The spirit lifted me up and bore me away; I went in bitterness in the heat of my spirit, the hand of the Lord being strong upon me. I came to the exiles at Tel-abib, who lived by the river Chebar. And I sat there among them, stunned, for seven days. (Ezek 3:14–15)

I am reminded of how Dr. Martin Luther King Jr. in an undelivered sermon once suggested that Ezekiel's prophetic action is a model for the way that white people can come to understand Black people and the struggles they face. We must all be willing to sit down together.[6] This can't happen overnight. For about six months people kept asking me, "Why are you here?" But eventually they came to understand why: because (I kept saying) God loves you, and so do I.

When white folks go to sit together with their brothers and sisters in Allendale, everybody grows. But the white folks will change in many ways. They see how hard it is for people like Isaiah, who couldn't find a job and who had to scratch for any opportunity to feed his kids. They start to ask hard questions: what if we can diminish the obstacles that get in the way of people thriving? Many of the people who visit are not able to stay a long time, and so we tell them to work in their own neighborhoods, reaching out to their own neighbors. I learned that love overcomes the obstacles of being a stranger, being from different socioeconomic levels, being different races. And love overcomes

---

[6] Martin Luther King Jr., "I Sat Where They Sat," in *The Papers of Martin Luther King, Jr.*, vol. 6, *Advocate of the Social Gospel, September 1948–March 1963*, ed. Clayborne Carson et al. (Berkeley and Los Angeles: University of California Press, 2007), 581.

fear! People today are afraid to even go next door, let alone a place like what Allendale used to be. But we can train people to overcome their fear in order to take the risk of loving others.

I understand that people today are afraid. I was afraid too. But what helped me to overcome my fear was obedience to the very message that I had been preaching for many years, that love overcomes fear. I had to understand whether it worked. And I'm here to tell you that it does.

Church Renewal

It was during that period of walking the streets that I joined Mount Canaan Missionary Baptist Church and met Pastor Harry Blake. He introduced me to other pastors and enabled me to build a network of people similarly committed to remaking the city. That network was the beginning of what was then called Church Renewal Ministries.

Both pastors and the leading families of various churches understood that decline in the city also meant the decline of congregations. So I began reaching out to some of these families, asking them to sponsor suppers where pastors—both Black and white—could gather together to think about renewal. The suppers were a hit. I asked them to share the funniest thing that happened to them in their ministry, just to give them a chance to laugh together. They got to know one another and build a sense of community. And they realized that they all had the same hopes for our community, and began to dream together. They organized pulpit exchanges and began to grow connections.

During this same time I reached out to the founding bishop of the Catholic Diocese of Shreveport, William Friend. I sensed that he would be an important ally in the work of renewal. Years earlier, while I was still a pastor in Texas, I had admired the work of the Catholic priests—they were always where the poorest folks lived, but they also seemed isolated in a region where they were a minority. I'd made a point of developing intentional friendship with the priests I met. I had also met the bishop of the Diocese of Amarillo, Leroy Matthiesen, who had joined other religious leaders in denouncing the manufacture of the neutron bomb at the nearby Pantex plant, and admired his courage in doing so.

I set up a lunch with Bishop Friend, and we hit it off. We set up a weekly lunch and got to be friends. Within a year he asked me to come share my plans for community renewal with his diocesan staff, and he then opened up to me every pulpit in his diocese. It was no small matter, I realized, for a Catholic bishop to invite a former Protestant pastor to speak in his churches. We grew very close over the following years, so much so that I asked him to be on our board when we first launched what has now become Community Renewal International.

2

Building a Movement

It did not take long to realize that even here in our part of the South, the "buckle of the Bible Belt," where churches are the backbone of the community, we needed to reach beyond our congregations to build a movement that would rebuild our entire community. But first I had to clarify how we were going to do that.

I took a two-day retreat at my own home, asking God and myself how to motivate a quarter of a million people—the population of Shreveport and Bossier City—to work together. I began with what was most evident, that we had to begin with the common human desire to love and to be loved in return. Almost immediately I also realized that we couldn't use tired, overworn "love" language, and so I focused on the word *caring* instead. Probably 99.9 percent of people are capable of caring for someone else, and it is possible, I thought, to enlist people's instinct to care for others in a connected way.

Over the course of that weekend I put together 121 index cards (which I still have), laying out the *system* of caring. Individual acts of caring aren't enough; we must work together to remake our world, block by block. And I understood that this system had to have the same kind of strategic vision that mobilizes armies to take first one block, then another, then another, until they have captured an entire city. That vision had to have accountability, leadership, and a shared conviction about what victory meant.

The key was identifying what was at the very foundation of society as a system of positive relationships, and building up that foundation through connected caring. I was persuaded by Toynbee's thesis that a creative minority could, through innovative responses to the challenges of their world, inspire among people a desire to imitate their way of being in the world. Our creative minority would be called the Renewal Team—a group of people who committed themselves to working together to remake the worlds they lived in. But if the renewal team itself was to get off the ground, we had to first commit to building good relationships among ourselves.

I was working on what I later called a "social technology," a way of describing the work or art (*techne*) of becoming a society. What would it look like, I asked, if we invested the same kind of time and attention in our social relationships as we did in our computer chips or other kinds of technology? How might our relationships improve as incrementally as our other kinds of technology?

Relationships Have Rules

Just as we have learned to improve our gadgetry incrementally and generationally, we can create a social technology that can be ever improved. Once we had Model T's; now we have the Tesla Model X. Every technology has intentionally, deliberately, and methodically lent itself to the process of improving performance both incrementally and generationally. Witness the history of the mobile phone! I believe that a similar social technology is now within both our reach and our grasp. Technology is nothing more than taking scientific principles and making them practically applicable through the use of tools. It is a way that we have of taking a concept and combining it with the right tool to produce the desired results. How do I fix my hair? I pick up a comb and slide it through. Something that was thought of long ago and then invented to achieve the desired results.

It is hard for us to think about the scientific principles that govern human relationships because we are so busy living within what, at times, is a bewildering blur of daily interactions that makes it difficult to step back and decipher what works and what doesn't. It is like the story a good friend of mine tells about the loving but mercurial friendship he and his wife of more than twenty-five years have: "Mack, we have fought so much that now I'll call her up and say, 'Honey, I am going to be late home from work tonight, so go ahead and start the argument without me!'"

Or, we think that if we get "scientific" about our relationships it will rob us of the richness of the relationship itself. We think it would feel like listening to a lecture on the nature and significance of human laughter without hearing one funny thing. But if we stop to think about our relationships, then, of course, we discover that they have very powerful and very critical rules. And if we obey these rules, then we grow in our friendships with one another and to our amazement find that we are fulfilled too. And if we disobey these rules, we find ourselves in increasing conflict, unhappiness, and isolation. Our growth is stunted.

Relationships have rules. I did at least know that. And when I remembered Toynbee's definition of society itself as a system of (positive) relationships, I knew that the human race had an answer for finding a way out of the quagmire of Lewis Mumford's characterization of the chief enigma of history . . . why do we keep collapsing the societies we construct?

The answer to Mumford is really very simple and therefore not an enigma at all. We must be disobeying the rules of human relationships, not just individually, but on a grand scale, on a societal or even global scale. Societal decay follows relational decay. What, then, are some of the rules that create positive relationships enabling all of us involved to grow and emotionally prosper in our souls? They are not a mystery. If you will reflect for just a moment, you will realize what it takes to be a friend and to have a friend. And you will also know what not to do to be a friend and to have a friend.

One primary rule about human relationships in general is that they are dynamic and always moving. You are either growing in closeness or you are diminishing in your relationships. It can be rapid or slow but never static. This rule leads to the relational rule of intentionality. We can meet each other incidentally and even accidentally, but we can only be friends intentionally. And this means that we must be conscious in cultivating our relationships by communicating (speaking and listening, thus sharing). Working together, belonging together, suffering together, laughing together, giving together, sacrificing together, all of these things and a thousand more make up the fundamental truth about human relationships. Positive relationships are based upon what we share in common. This is the symphony of life. It is when different instruments make the same song and the music fills us all.

Diversity training has its rightful place, but we can never take the path of extolling diversity expecting to arrive at the destination of unity. This fact stands: we are each unique. We are uniquely unrepeated and unrepeatable creatures. There never has been another you, and there never will be another you. So we now have nearly eight billion distinct human personalities. And we are therefore infinitely diverse and increasingly so. The key to unifying relationships is to recognize and celebrate our endearing differences, which are transcended by what we share in common. Each person is precious. What a great reality—to share much together in common as human beings!

So even though we are all distinct from one another with an unbounded urge to be unique, there is also within us the profound instinct to be together. It is precisely here that political systems have sought to express that reality. Each time in history that the balance between uniqueness and unity was not struck, lifting both instincts, something monstrously destructive was birthed, from anarchy to totalitarianism.

I used to counsel premarital couples. They would come into my office positively giddy with love and filled with expectation. I always would begin by saying, "Now, I have good news for you and bad news. The good news is that God has laid down rules that have to do with your relationship, and if you obey those rules, God has promised that the 'two of you will become one.' Now here is the bad news: you are about to embark on a lifelong struggle to see which one of you the two of you are going to become."

Even positive relationships can become bruised or even broken. We know that. We have all experienced the hurt and even the tragedy of that sad state. We have been both victim and perpetrator. But we also know that if we follow certain rules, then just like our broken bones, broken souls can be healed, and so can bruised or broken relationships. Through years of experience I have seen hurting hearts become whole again, and I have seen gaping relational wounds cleansed and sewed up and made well.

Of course, we know that acknowledging our failures and seeking forgiveness—as well as forgiving the hurts we have actually experienced—move our relationships to stronger and stronger ground. In the marriage ceremony we declare that we will take the one we love "for better or for worse, for richer or for poorer, in sickness and in health, to love and to cherish until we are parted by death." That really should be the covenant of every friendship. We cannot grow without commitment!

Every now and then I would have people say to me, "Preacher, I'm with you as long as you're right!" I always wanted to reply, "Hey, don't do me any favors! I won't need you when I'm right. It is when I have messed up, and am off track, and unhappy, and wrong, and just a mess myself, that I desperately need you." When we say or commit to "for better or worse," we just don't know and cannot know what that will mean or bring. But by and by, as we have stuck together as friends by celebrating all of our "for betters" and clung to and forgiven one another all of our "for worses," our relationship takes on a strength and a bond that becomes prodigious. We do not know what tomorrow will bring to a friendship, but we do know that our friendship is a tower built of all the "for better" bricks and held together by all of the "for worse" mortar. Relationships have rules.

The centrality of human relationships for all of us is also illustrated by the fact that relationships can be the source of terrible suffering and dysfunction. Just as we all know the power of caring and loving friendships, we are also fully aware of the destructive ability of negative relationships, whether within our own families or in the world about us. Abusive relationships have power, too. They can emotionally cripple us for life. They can make us insane, and even rob us of the capacity to go on living.

Think of the dark power of rejection and remember the suicides of our young folks in the face of bullying or derisive scorn.

When I read Toynbee's words, my whole experience rose up to greet me with an affirmation that the one common denominator for all of human living lies within the reality we call relationships. And therefore, if we repeatedly continue the cycle of societal disintegration, it must be because our relationships are disintegrating. And that must be because we are not walking in the rules whereby we build positive relationships that have the power to grow us.

Society is a system of positive relationships. Think of that for a moment. As I wrote, at that time in 1981, I surely grasped the relationships part of that statement, but I was still clueless about the part about a "system." If Toynbee was right, I reasoned, the entire nature of society is composed of various systems rolled into one system of relationships, both good and bad, positive and negative. Therefore, we had to find a system that could exponentially increase the number of positive relationships in the world today. This could be a system that surely may not come to pass within my lifetime or yours, but we could create a blueprint for such a system, lay the foundations for its construction, and pass the plans and building on to the next generations for their work and improvements in the model. By this means we could begin to leaven the world's population in a system of intentional and methodical renewing of human community. How to grow the system?

It was clear that in order to have a better world we must have better people. But what does "better" mean and how do we begin to become better as human beings? If we could answer that, then the shared hope of the ages for a world that is renewed and ever renewing relationally could be within the grasp of the human race. So we began to develop a system to produce positive relationships. What a difference this could make! It means that we could grow better people and a better society all at once, together, at the same time.

We started with the tiniest component of that system as our primary goal. How do we grow better people? Ask a common farmer, one who has farmed all of his life, "How does a corn seed grow?" and the likelihood of him providing the biological/ biochemical process integral to a seed's growth is negligible. Go even further, for him to give an accurate answer to the mystery of life itself would be rather unusual, too. But ask him how to grow corn seeds and he will share the certainty of experienced convictions and behavior. He will share with profound knowledge of both the conditions necessary for growth as well as the steps to take in order that it will happen. Not knowing how corn seeds grow does not prevent our farmer from growing corn in ever-increasing abundance and quality.

So too with growing people. There abides a mystery that perhaps we will never unlock regarding the processes whereby friendship grows us from within, but grow us it does. Just as Socrates helped all of us to see truth through the prism of right questions, so we set out in our own baby-step way to frame questions that would lead us to the door of systems of relationships. We asked:

- What kind of a world do we need?
- What kind of society makes possible that kind of world?
- What kind of person makes possible that kind of society?
- What kind of conditions produce those kinds of persons?
- What do we have to do to make those conditions possible?

We answered simply:

- We need a world that is a home where every single person can grow up safe and loved.
- We need a society guided by the primacy of the preciousness of every single human being without exception.
- We need this society to be filled with whole persons.

These whole persons are produced by caring relationships of ever growing friendships. But we didn't have the slightest idea how to produce those conditions!

So while we staggered forward in producing a system, our thesis for whatever system was to arise was quite simple: better people make a better society and positive relationships are the conditions that produce better people in abundance, thus producing a better society. And once we found a method for that to occur, even if very rudimentary at the outset, then improving the method would lead to an exponential increase in results. The results of better people and societies, then, mean that the conditions increase for a more optimum environment resulting in better and better growth over time.

A Swimming Pool

Let me give an example. I remembered when I was younger having to clean my uncle's swimming pool by hand, emptying it entirely and tediously having to scrub it down again and again. It was a Sisyphean task! It had no filtering system.

How, I pondered, do you make an entire Olympic-size swimming pool healthy enough for people to swim? Well, you must know what it takes to remove the dust speck from one molecule of H_2O. If you do not know that, then no matter what elaborate lengths you may employ to make the pool healthy will not work. You must know what will remove the dust from one molecule of water. But if that is all you know, then you still will not be successful in making the pool fit to inhabit. It will continue to cause disease.

Rather than emptying all of the dirty water out of the pool and then refilling it with healthy water, a temporary but really dumb process, someone invented a system called a swimming-pool filter. This system was able to draw in billions of water molecules, send them through the efficient process necessary to remove dust specks from the molecules, and then send them out in such volume and velocity that would overwhelm the dusty molecules' ability to contaminate. Given time, the process would eventually make the pool healthy enough to swim in.

Next, the system was replicated worldwide, and now we can renew every pool no matter what size using the technological formula and application found in swimming-pool filters. And think of the incremental and generational improvement. Today we can make the filters smaller and more efficient to the extent that we can even drink what was once forbidden for swimming. We even have news of a nanotechnology whereby salt water can be made drinkable by using a one-atom-thick reverse osmosis process. Talk about technological progress!

You don't just clean a section of a swimming pool. And you cannot just clean the area in which you and your friends and family swim. That is obvious with water. It is interconnected and dynamic, so the whole body of water must be addressed. And what is obvious with water must also become obvious to the relational world—the pool of humanity. We keep scrubbing molecules because we concentrate on the social atom—thinking erroneously that eventually we will be successful in cleaning the pool. We know intuitively that we must address the individual within society, or even identifiable sections of the pool, but we are stuck in a repetitive cycle of failure because our efforts are largely unrelated, uncoordinated, and nonsequential: the exact opposite of an efficient swimming pool filtering system. We have wonderful and effective nonprofits, government agencies, organizations, and institutions, all in the atom scrubbing business and all showing great results. But the pool is not becoming healthier.

We know that the pool of humanity is made up of the "people atoms" entering into relationships, thus making up the human race, just as the swimming-pool atoms combine into molecules called H_2O and thus composing the reality of the world of water. But in the absence of an integrating system producing the healthy relational molecules en masse, we will continue to repeat history now with ever-increasing devastation.

Our Social Technology

What began as Shreveport Community Renewal in 1994 had to plant and multiply friendships with citywide intentionality. And I must point out here that this did not mean that everyone had to try to be friends with everyone in the whole city. I always spoke of the example of a brick wall. In usual construction methods the bricklayer so offsets the bricks that each brick laid and mortared in only touches six other bricks. But it is still connected by the mortar and the bricks it touches to every other brick in the wall. And so it is with each of us. We rarely have more than a handful of close friends, yet we must see that we are connected to everyone by the common commitments we are living by and with.

We could effectively produce a practical model that could begin systematically to grow better people, resulting in the communitywide increase in positive functionality and a convincing decrease in citywide societal dysfunction. And if we could discover a way to measure both the micro (better people) and the macro (better cities) results, then we could with confidence show that by finding a way to delineate and deepen positive relationships, we could change lives and therefore whole cities for the good. We then would be ready to replicate the system for every other city on the globe.

The great urban designer Daniel Burnham shatteringly observed over a century ago, with Chicago in his heart: "Make no small plans. They have no magic to stir men's blood and probably themselves will not be realized. Make big plans; aim high in hope and work, remembering that a noble, logical diagram once recorded will never die, but long after we are gone will be a living thing, asserting itself with ever-growing insistency."[1] Echoing this sentiment, we marched out to strategically and tactically regrow the foundations of community itself.

I remembered three ingredients that the Romans had used to invent cement, which led to the most incredible architectural breakthroughs imaginable. They took lime, sand, and water, and they stirred them together, making a material that over time continued to harden until it was stronger than granite itself! So we took three methods in our approach to lay the foundations for a whole city connected together again. And remember, our goal was to cultivate the elements of the village within a city—what I call "re-village-izing"—in order to create the caring environment necessary to produce whole persons. We called them the Renewal Team, Haven House, and Friendship House.

---

[1] Daniel Burnham, "Stirred by Burnham, Democracy Champion," *Chicago Record-Herald*, October 15, 1910.

Part Two

Focusing on Essentials

3

Combining the Three Ingredients

Our first move was to establish the Renewal Team, which we imagined as a movement of people across the city who committed themselves to caring. The Renewal Team includes businesses and organizations, but the majority are individuals in the We Care Team—men and women from all walks of life who commit themselves to making caring visible. If you are a member of the human race, then you are a part of the whole, whether you want to be or not! So, according to the rules of positive relationships, we reasoned, in order to be concretely connected together, we must find what we share together in common. This meant that our differences can be wonderfully celebrated but at the same time our differences would be transcended by our shared commonality.

We have in our city all kinds of ethnic and cultural backgrounds. We have rich and poor. We have young and old. We have male and female. We have educated and uneducated. We have all of the religious differences you can imagine. We draw members of the many Baptist, Catholic, Methodist, and nondenominational churches in town, but also B'nai Zion, a Reform Jewish congregation, and Agudath Achim, the Conservative congregation. We also attract people from all walks of life who are not affiliated with any congregation. So what does all of that illustrated and real diversity share in common for heaven's sake? I believe that we share as human beings the capacity to care for one another. But I also believe that if you are a normal person, then you have the capacity to care.

Having the capacity to care doesn't mean that we have actualized all of the potential to care for one another. No human being living today has really reached his or her potential to care for others. And all kinds of conditions serve to keep us from fully actualizing our capacity, but nonetheless, we reasoned that 99 percent of our neighbors had the capacity to care for others to some degree. Therefore, only a very small number of folks did not have that capacity. We call them psychopathic or sociopathic personalities. (Again, fascinatingly enough, one of my neurosurgeon friends tells me that they haven't been able to find mirror neurons in the brain of the psychopath.)

So we set out rightly assuming, I believe, that the overwhelmingly vast majority of human beings want to help one another, while a minuscule minority seemingly wants others to hurt. The problem before us is that we did not have a way to find the majority of normal folks. They were hidden from us and each other precisely because of their common normality! Usually the terribly dysfunctional make the news. That is because news projects the anomalous of life and not its normalness. Normal folks just go about their everyday living, helping one another almost unconsciously. And what is the reality of caring in every city is hidden. It is real. But it is largely invisible to the collective consciousness of the city itself.

Catastrophe surfaces caring people. Let a catastrophic event occur and all of sudden, what was real within the people of the city, that is, caring for one another, becomes massively visible. We rise to help. When the tragedy of September 11, 2001, hit New York City, it did not change the New Yorkers from cold to caring. That catastrophe merely revealed them. And they poured forth to aid and support and enwrap one another in their normal caring ways that just appeared extraordinary. It was quite ordinary, only now the caring was visible to all. What had been the nature of the people of the city was there all along and functioning below the collective consciousness of the city and the world. But catastrophe and need peel back the covers and allow us to see that the real has become visible. Once the catastrophic recedes, then little, by little by degrees, the caring slips back down to the everyday and ceases to be seen in the large eye of the public. Caring is normal. And it is what normal people share in common.

But how to surface caring people actively instead of waiting for a catastrophe and how to stay continually surfaced were the questions. We knew that once we could make caring people visible to one another on a citywide scale and then maintain that visibility, a psychological and emotional connection could be made as a first step to deepening our shared humanity. All movements begin with this step whereby a transcendent commonality is recognized and joined. And so becoming visible to one another in our shared commitments is the step that can lead to deepening connection to one another and then to committing together to bring our transcendent cause to reality for all.

The We Care Team

We devised an "I Care" card that asked people to fill out their name, address, and contact information, and then we asked for something new. We asked them to share just one thing they were already doing to help others. Then they were to take the We Care pin attached to the card and wear it. They were also to take the We Care bumper sticker attached to the card and put it on their car. And, if they wanted to place a We Care yard sign in their yard or in the window of their apartment, they were to let us know that too. And finally, they needed to let us know if they wanted to become connected to one another by receiving a newsletter bringing all sorts of positive stories about caring on the individual and group scales in our *Renewal News*. Of course, one can easily see that we were moving to create a paradigm shift by changing the perception of our environment to one of positive functionality based upon the reality of the vastness of caring, in contrast to the regular news cycles, which feature human dysfunction.

Using individual networks as well as all kinds of group gatherings from faith groups, to businesses, schools, clubs, and organizations, and continuing to expand and nourish those human rivers, we have grown the We Care Team in Shreveport and Bossier City to tens of thousands of card-signing folks. (We have the cards to prove it!) We will continue to grow this number so that everyone in the city will regularly encounter signs, bumper stickers, and pins that remind them of our shared commitment to caring. These daily reminders will make people visible to one another, and therefore aware that together we are the biggest gang in town.

The Renewal Team and specifically the We Care Team embrace everyone within the city limits. Note that our card only asked for name, connection information, and that one caring act they were already doing to help others. We did not surface diversity, whether gender, ethnicity, nationality, faith, socioeconomic status, or age, because relationships are formed by what we share in common. And caring is the most common and connecting capacity that we human beings possess.

But we needed to do more than just surface and therefore see the caring reality of the people of our city. That is only one element of the social cement. We also needed to rebuild the connections of caring people where they lived. If an army is to capture a city without its utter destruction, then it must do so street by street, dwelling by dwelling. And so it was with our caring army. We had to engage and cultivate the elements of a village in our cities by going down to the neighbor level. With only a comparatively few exceptions, we all live somewhere. And those who have no dwelling among us must be cared for or we are not caring. It is as simple as that.

Haven House

The larger task of rebuilding the foundations of an entire populace means that we must give our attention also to those who do inhabit some dwelling where they live. This necessity gave rise to the second ingredient in the social cement mix, which we call Haven House.

What if we could get a whole group of people to go to the places where they live and get to know their neighbors and be a catalyst for helping their neighbors get to know one another? I pondered the potential. Those obstacles that I had encountered when I went down to Lawrence Street, which seemed to loom so large, could be eclipsed. We might not know our neighbors, but we are not strangers because they see us every now and then coming and going. And it is an unfortunate reality—which needs to change in our nation—that we are usually the same ethnicity as the majority of the people who live around us.

We also are usually on a socioeconomic par with most of our neighbors. And while we might have the natural fear of meeting our neighbors "cold," so to speak, if we were trained to do so with a reason for doing it, then the fear would be diminished enough to be overcome. When I grew up in Shreveport, I lived in the same house on the same street from the time that my parents brought me home from the hospital after my birth until I married. And growing up on East Fairview, I knew every single person on my street. I knew who lived in all twenty-four houses, and they all knew me. We were a village in the midst of a city. And we were connected as neighbors all helping one another. I remember Hesiod, the ancient Greek sage, proclaiming that neighbors will rush to our aid in bedclothes even when our relatives are dawdling over what to wear.[1]

Where are we today? We can message people all over the world all of the time. And when we go home to our house or our apartment, we don't know who is living and dying just across the street.

Haven House provides another way to systematize our positive relationships on a citywide basis. We begin to recruit volunteers and train them in a one-hour session with others who have volunteered to be Haven House leaders, and then we send them back to their homes with a plan and a method to reach out and get to know their neighbors and then help their neighbors get to know one another. It is reconnecting the people based upon their common capacity to care. We have now trained over seventeen hundred Haven House leaders citywide. These are folks from every walk of life, ethnicity, and social level, and they are

---

[1] Hesiod, *Works and Days*, trans. Apostolos N. Athanassakis (Baltimore: Johns Hopkins University Press, 2004), lines 344–45: "If misfortune strikes your house, neighbors will come in their bedclothes; kinsmen will dress up."

working together in the common cause of caring. The task of the Haven House leader is simply to be a friend and help people get to be friends with one another. So the training is easy. Find out who lives around you by inviting everyone over for a party. Why have a meeting when you can have a party? So we unite together not based upon anything but getting to be friends and maintaining those friendships.

Learning from the Ants

By 1996 our plans for the first two ingredients in remaking our city were taking root, and we could devote ourselves to planning how to develop the third ingredient. An insight came when I turned on the television to the Discovery Channel and the screen was filled with a blob of ants. There were only about two minutes left in the show, so I watched until it was over and I could see the next hour's presentation, which I was eagerly awaiting. Something about dinosaurs, I think. Within a few seconds I was sitting bolt upright in the rocking chair.

The narrator said something that almost knocked the wind out of me. "Ants solve sophisticated problems with very simple solutions repeated over and over." That got my attention in a big way, and I started paying attention to the blob of ants on the television. The voice went on to explain the activities of the ants before me. I watched for two minutes. Then I did something that I had never done before. I picked up the phone and called the 800 number on the screen. I gave them my sacred Visa card number and ordered the $19.95 video, shipping and handling extra.

I know that that video doesn't sound too toe-tappingly exciting. But when I tell you what I saw, I know that you will agree with me that those ants were exciting. What was the two-minute drill about renewal in that video?

The ants in the picture were being treated like laboratory mice. Scientists had placed a colony of them on a plain, flat surface that was not conducive to the construction of a secure nest at all. The ants had plenty of sand grains around, but the ants were in trouble. They were exposed and vulnerable on that surface. (Remember: ants are not known for having large brains. But remember something else: ants have constructed successful societies for millions of years.)

Then the scientists placed a rod from the plain surface and connected it to a surface that contained an ideal environment for the building of a nest. It looked like a keyhole laid flat on the table. It was perfect to house the colony and to blockade the narrow opening for protection. The connecting rod was only one ant wide. Then we watched.

A single ant began to tentatively cross the rod. It reached the new surface and began to explore every facet of the keyhole-like nesting area. Its feelers were thoroughly adept at touching every millimeter of surface area. When it had completed its reconnaissance, it crossed back over the bridge to the milling colony. Then it did something absolutely astonishing. The first ant picked up another ant and carried it bodily over the bridge to the new area. Together they repeated the survey of the potential nest area. They both then returned across the rod, single file, and they each picked up another ant and carried those ants across. Now there were four. All explored in a now familiar pattern. Over and over the process repeated itself. There were no variations on this theme.

At some point enough ants had been carried bodily that some critical mass had been reached and the flow began where each member of the colony started across the bridge, every ant following another. But now they had grains of sand in their pincers. They settled into the large round area of the "keyhole" and began to place the grains of sand over the narrow entrance, affording them a protected and secure place to live.

I watched in wonder. In the space of two minutes a huge problem facing the little-bitty-brained ants was given a sophisticated solution: the colony was mobilized and marched together to a new land where the members rapidly constructed a safe place for themselves. They did this by using a simple act and repeating it over and over and over until they changed the situation.

You can see why I sat straight up and took notice. This is precisely the premise we believe lies at the heart of societal change for us. We believe and are absolutely dedicated to the proposition that the only way complex social problems can be solved is through the repetitive rebuilding of the molecular structure of society itself. By building and growing positive, caring relationships in a systematic way, society itself can be renewed. This is the formula: a simple act put into a repetitive system solves a sophisticated challenge.

It also means that we can never solve the complexities of the massive problems facing us by a frontal assault. The problems of crime, drugs, family disintegration, joblessness, poverty, and racism can never be solved by the think-tank approach alone. By studying the problem and theorizing its solution one simply encounters a dysfunctional social Rubik's cube where each solution brings new variables.

I am utterly convinced that Jesus was right when he said that the kingdom of heaven is like a woman who took a little leaven and mixed it into a large amount of flour until all the dough was leavened (Mt 13:33; Lk 13:20–21). I believe that the leavening process of repetitive acts of intentional and systematized caring will create an environment in which we can live in safe and nurturing neighborhoods. I believe that is the only way that society can be restored. It is the warp and the woof of God's universe. It is one ant carrying another ant. It is one person carrying another. That is the only way it works.

When I finished watching that show, I remembered a strange passage of scripture. I knew that it was in Proverbs, but I did not remember where. Then I found it. Proverbs 6:6 says:

> Go to the ant, you lazybones;
>   consider its ways, and be wise.

If each block had a Haven House leader who was repetitively building friendships among and between neighbors, then, like the ants, we would rebuild our city for our children and their children. We would watch crime fall, drugs cease, families come together, work increase, abundance shared, and love for all abound. We have already seen this happening in Shreveport and Bossier City.

Care Clusters

Today, we have all of our Haven House leaders meet in assigned groups of twenty called Care Clusters. The meetings are kept positive by sharing all of the good things going on where they live and encouraging one another in a fifty-five minute meeting. Once a year, all of the leaders gather for our annual citywide sharing and celebration of our Haven House leaders. It is a revolution in hope and joy! Just love where you live! But do it together, intentionally and systematically. We even have a slogan, because no revolution can succeed without a simple slogan to tie the common person to a transcendent cause. Our slogan: "We are remaking our city by making friends on our street or in our apartments."

Just imagine covering every city street and every apartment floor with dedicated volunteers who reach out to connect with their neighbors and help their neighbors connect with one another. Also imagine those who are leading this effort on each street and in every apartment complex united with one another in the high cause of actively caring for their neighbors through friendship. It is simply an ancient solution to a modern need: we are remaking village life in the twenty-first-century city. We do have some clear rules for those we train in order to make sure that the quality of our commitment to caring goes forward with strength of purpose. Most important is that Haven House leaders never advertise for a political campaign. This strategy ensures that they stay focused on the relational foundation of their neighborhoods, the foundation that can then give rise to a more relational public conversation.

4

The Need for
Friendship Houses

In 1997, Community Renewal launched the third ingredient, Friendship Houses, in the areas of the highest crime and greatest poverty in our city. This very intense strategy called for a bold and sacrificial step. To be friends, we reasoned, meant that we must go and be with our friends. We had to invite those with resources to help us build homes in order to organize generous people to live together in broken neighborhoods if we were to make both the rich and the poor whole. This was breaking new ground, because one fundamental rule of life is that every creature reproduces after its own kind. If we could go and live with our brothers and sisters, we could be a living link within a caring relationship that could be a lifeline to the world of wholeness. But taking that step meant that we first had to find the funding.

Clarence Jordan, the scholar who was a mentor to Millard Fuller, the founder of Habitat for Humanity (whom I'll talk about later), used to say it very well: "What the poor need is not charity but capital, not caseworkers but coworkers. And what the rich need is a wise, honorable, and just way of divesting themselves of their overabundance."[1]

Our thinking called for us to rehabilitate existing houses in the neighborhood or construct new houses in that designated area of ten blocks. Two community coordinators would then move into the houses with their families and begin to reconnect the people who lived in the neighborhood through their common capacity to care for one another. We planned to have each ten-square-block area leavened in this way. The coordinators could work as a team to regrow intentional caring for the neighborhood. In effect, their job was to place their arms around that neighborhood in an embrace of loving kindness and not let go.

Two Kinds of Poverty

As we look at our cities, we cannot help but see that there are areas of decay that are stark reminders that prospects for many of our fellow citizens are massively hindered by their captivity in poverty. Not only are they bound by the limits of their poverty, but they are further chained in areas where crime and poor health conditions become the iron links and locks on those chains. They are trapped. The caring infrastructure within these areas is under siege and is only steps away from full collapse. Our traditional answer to these brothers and sisters has been to lob just enough services over the wall that they can survive but not enough to escape. I am convinced that our massive social service paradigm has an elaborately contrived system that maintains a symbiotic relationship with societal pathology. It is as if we built

---

[1] In David Snell, "The History and Future of Partnership Housing," in *Roots in the Cotton Patch: The Clarence Jordan Symposium 2012*, vol. 2, ed. Kirk Lyman-Barner and Cori Lyman-Barner (Eugene, OR: Cascade Books, 2014), 90.

a massive hospital with thousands of well-meaning workers at the foot of a cliff where adults and children regularly fall, with pitiable consequences. Why not build a fence at the cliff's edge instead? Our social service world mostly dwells at the foot of society's cliff. We keep pathology alive as we stay in business. But we don't cure it.

I must also add that the poor are quite visible. But if we look with real eyes at our cities, there is a class of people that we usually miss. That is the class of those who are impoverished in their exercise of true empathy for their fellows.[2] Books have been written about the psychology of poverty and the pathology of the idle poor, but not nearly as much study has been given to the psychology of wealth as has been given to all of the need assessments through the teeming neighborhoods of the poor. We need to study the psychology of the idle rich equally as much, if not more.[3] As we drive we can see young men in groups loitering on corners or lounging on porches, and we want to scream, "Get a job!" But when we drive through the streets of the very rich, we can't see them. We can only see gates that block driveways that curve off out of sight. We can't see them because they are

---

[2] See Lynn Twist, *The Soul of Money: Transforming Your Relationship with Money and Life* (New York: W. W. Norton, 2017). In this book the author describes a meeting with Mother Teresa. She describes Mother Teresa's reflection on an ugly incident with a wealthy couple: "The vicious cycle of poverty, she said, has been clearly articulated and is widely known. What is less obvious and goes almost completely unacknowledged is the vicious cycle of wealth. There is no recognition of the trap wealth so often is, and of the suffering of the wealthy: the loneliness, the isolation, the hardening of the heart, the hunger and the poverty of the soul that can come with the burden of wealth" (35).

[3] Some studies suggest that wealth can reduce empathy, cloud moral judgment, make people vulnerable to addiction and depression, and harm well-being. For an overview, see Carolyn Gregoire, "How Money Changes the Way You Think and Feel," *Huffington Post*, January 6, 2014.

loitering in groups at clubs, or on yachts, or in private jets, or lounging in penthouses.

My friend Paige Hoffpauir, a regular volunteer with Community Renewal and a member of our board of directors, tells a story that is both evidence of the ills that can afflict the rich and also hope for how they too might be transformed through the encounters that Friendship Houses make possible. Decades ago Paige was a successful real-estate broker who lived in one of the most affluent neighborhoods in Shreveport. She found her life lacked meaning; her ambitions and pursuit of wealth left her feeling empty and without purpose. So she sought out an opportunity to do charity work and learned about Community Renewal. That encounter helped her to discover that, in her words, "I was the charity!" She came to a realization that she had never really learned to love her neighbors in any meaningful way, and so she began a journey of personal transformation by trying to make friends on her block. What she discovered is that there were many like her who were hungry for connection, and that the ordinary patterns of life in her neighborhood did not afford opportunity for it.

There are many wealthy people who are depleted within their souls. This is why Walter Rauschenbusch, the trumpet of America's great social awakening at the turn of the nineteenth century, wrote in his book *A Theology for the Social Gospel* that money was "soul poison." We must think through more effective means to free our imprisoned brothers and sisters. I have seen how love and helping to love and serve one another sets us free. But to free the wealthy from the traps of this master, that is coldly unrelenting in its capacity to suck vitality and meaningful living, begins with a powerful commitment of friendship. Our goal with Friendship Houses was to dedicate resources in a way that allowed for the friendship of rich and poor to grow organically.

It is not transactional, like professional/client or even helper/ helpee. Friends are equal in both giving and receiving, and both are changed for the better and grow in their competence and compassion as they walk together. The Friendship House called upon us to commit to be friends consciously knowing that we, too, would be changed unconsciously.

Community Coordinators

It was during this period that we began to meet some remarkable human beings who were invited to spearhead this transformational approach. I invited them to make the commitment to be trained, funded, and sent to live on a full-time basis in our highest crime and highest poverty neighborhoods.

We were not very scientific. We didn't do a needs assessment, simply because we were convinced that what we all needed was to give and receive love. We also believed that the best vehicle for meeting this fundamental need that we all shared was the restoration of the village infrastructure. This meant that the fundamentals of the village were everyone's needs. We just chose the highest crime areas in the city and moved in to live. To us, it was a revolution.

But our revolution was ignited by firmly believing and stepping out on the commitment that friendship was the medium through which all of our needs would be met. So our primary task was to give ourselves to our neighbors in friendship. We thought that we could rebuild the caring infrastructure in those devastated neighborhoods by selecting a ten square block area and restore the village conductive power to the lives of those who lived within through rebuilding the intentional caring foundation upon which to stand.

The first task in rebuilding a culture of caring is to win trust. And the fundamental way of winning trust is to serve others. This must not be rooted in what C. S. Lewis has called "need love." Need love, he said, even while it is part of our very nature, can sometimes turn selfish.[4] If that is the basis of our commitment, then it will be both manipulative and frustrating. Our community coordinators went to live in those high crime areas in the midst of poverty that was pounding every day, with their spouses and children, because they were committed to serve, not expecting anything in return. This is a vital principle!

We are not a service provider. Others do that wonderfully well. But that was not our conviction, strategy, or calling. We came to be friends, and friends help each other because they love each other. They seek each other's good exactly as they seek their own good. C. S. Lewis describes us with his naming of another kind of love. He called it "gift love." Gift love means that you give expecting nothing in return.[5] Our community coordinators moved in to give the gift of themselves.

The Story of Barksdale Annex

Bossier City is the home of the famous Barksdale Air Force Base. During the Cold War it was the headquarters of the Strategic Air Command, and it housed the majority of the B-52 bomber fleet. It still does. When 9/11 exploded, it was from this base that President Bush first addressed the nation, having flown there from Florida for security's sake. Today there is a sign in front of the base that reads, "To Serve and To Protect." In 2002, I went

---

[4] C. S. Lewis, *The Four Loves* (San Francisco: HarperOne, 2017), 2.
[5] Lewis, 8.

to the mayor of Bossier City, and said: "Mayor Dement, we are now ready to bring the Friendship House to Bossier City, and we always pick the highest crime area. Where do you want us?" Without even so much as a blink, he answered, "The Barksdale Annex!"

The Barksdale Annex was absolutely notorious. It was an isolated enclave that was reached by literally crossing to the other side of the tracks; that is, the railroad that ran in front of Barksdale Air Force Base and also the Barksdale Annex. It was so dangerous in that neighborhood that it was the seat of most of Bossier City's violent crime. There were no pizza deliveries there. No cab would venture in to answer a call. And it was absolutely off limits to every airman on the Air Force base. It backed up to the base as the closest neighbor and was separated by only a large ditch and a chain-link fence. How ironic was this? Our major nuclear bomber arm, which was there at Barksdale Air Force Base to serve and to protect America, was off limits to its adjoining American neighbor. Those airmen needed protection from us?

We purchased a large lot in the neighborhood and gathered to break ground for the construction of our fifth Friendship House in our third neighborhood. With many friends, board members, and dignitaries, including Mayor Dement and Bishop Friend, we broke ground and dedicated the lot. Bishop Friend prayed a wonderful prayer of consecration, and then I got up to speak. As I talked, I looked over the heads of the crowd. There, across the street in front of a ramshackle house, was the scariest group of young men I had seen up to that point. They were doing some kind of hand jive that I came to learn were gang identification hand signals. I was worried.

As was our custom, we were led in a song by our Haven House director, Russell Minor, "Thank You, Lord!" As we were singing, to Mayor Dement's eternal embarrassment, one of the gang members came running across the street and then through the crowd screaming, "All of you m—- f———-s are going to die!" Was this an actual threat? It didn't seem to be. We carried on, dedicating what has now become our standard Friendship House: a large two-story house that has a large community room on one side of the first floor. This room contains not only a spacious room for groups from the neighborhood to use, but also a full kitchen, restroom, and office space for our community coordinator. On the other side of the first-floor wall, through a connecting door, is the family room, kitchen, and half-bath that the community coordinator and family use. Upstairs are four bedrooms and two full baths. It is a wonderful house with huge and inviting front and back porches for the community coordinator's family and, most important, the neighborhood to use.

When we were almost finished with the construction, we received word that the gang was going to intimidate our community coordinator, Tina Sheffield, so that she would be too frightened to move into the Barksdale Annex. One night they shot out all of the windows on the bottom floor, and soon the local television stations were on the way. I got to the Friendship House in time to see the cameras already rolling and sweeping back and forth from shattered windows to a river of glass littering the floors. Tina was about to be interviewed by reporters. With lights blazing and microphones in her face, the first questions that came were: "You are about to move into the most dangerous neighborhood in Bossier City, aren't you? And last night they shot out all of your windows. How do you feel about that?" I was behind the cameras, and I had the irresistible urge to leap over those guys and intervene by declaring: "That is not a fair question to ask in the immediate wake of this despicable act of cowardice and intimidation. Just look at the bullet holes! How do you think she's going to feel?" Mercifully, I was saved by her rapid and firm and even-tempered response.

Tina, a decorated veteran of the Air Force, said, "How do I feel? Why, that is why we are moving here. If the neighborhood was safe, then they wouldn't need us to be their friends." The reporters and I, and everybody else, were speechless. There just wasn't anything else to say in the face of that granite courage. We all just shut our open mouths and blinked several times as if to shake away the full blast of love that had just hit us flush in the face.

When the crowd was gone, I went to Tina and asked her what kind of fence she wanted for her and her family's protection. When she looked at me and said, "Mack, we don't need any kind of fence. I want everyone to feel welcome!" I knew we were on the side that wins. Friendship Houses like Tina's cost us about $340,000 to construct, and they are built in such impoverished areas that when they are finished, they usually plummet in value financially. But the value to the inspiration of precious souls in the neighborhoods is simply incalculable. So when we dedicate those houses, we always have a large gathering of the neighbors and make a point of saying exactly how much the house has cost. Then I say: "But the cost of the house does not compare to how precious you are. You are so worth it and more! Look under the house. There are no wheels. We have come to stay."

How important is that principle: we do not come by day and leave by night; we do not lob services over the wall and then go rest our arms. That is why I have described our community coordinators and their families as remarkable human beings. They move in to stay. Tina and Lonzo Sheffield are still living in the Friendship House in the Barksdale Annex. The gang is gone. Crime has dropped 48 percent. Pizzas are now delivered. Cabs come and go. And new houses by Habitat for Humanity have been built there.

Robert Handy, one of our volunteers who grew up in Allendale, speaks eloquently about what makes the Friendship House different from other government-funded programs that popped up from time to time in his neighborhood. The money would fund some brief program, get used, and then life would return to normal. What Robert saw in the Friendship House was a clear message: these people are here to stay. These are our new neighbors. So over time, he got involved. Today he's passing on the same commitment to others, giving of himself the way that he saw our community coordinators giving to the families living in his neighborhood. And there are many others like him.

Friendship is a transforming reality. We now have ten Friendship Houses in five neighborhoods, and as I write we are breaking ground on yet another that I'll describe later in this book. Since 1996, we have poured over fourteen million dollars into the most broken neighborhoods of Shreveport and Bossier through programs and personnel flowing out of the Friendship House into the streets of the city. Love with skin on it! Our goal is to have Friendship Houses in every high-need neighborhood. We start to restore the foundation of caring by winning trust. We win trust by serving. And we start by serving the most precious possessions of the neighborhood itself, the children and the youth.

Michael's Story

Michael Jackson was one of the first young people that I met during my early walks through Allendale. He had grown up there and was twelve years old at the time, living with his mother and grandmother amid the violence and drugs that were still common. As a teenager in the early 1990s, he was scarcely aware of the larger forces that had shaped the neighborhood. All around him was poverty: decrepit houses, abandoned businesses, unkempt parks. After coming to a Haven House rally, he was drawn to Community Renewal and eventually, as an adult, became himself a Haven House leader. Reflecting on those experiences, the word he uses most often is *positivity*—he saw that in our activities as a stark contrast to all the negativity that surrounded him in the neighborhood.

After we built the first Friendship House in Allendale, Michael became involved in the afterschool programs, where he met people who helped him to imagine a future and a way to use his gifts. Unlike many of his friends who ended up on drugs, in jail, or dead, Michael began to see a life beyond Allendale and was encouraged by the adults who were providing a model of how to live for others. He graduated from high school, earned a bachelor's degree, and then a law degree. Today, he works at a consulting firm in Shreveport and is active in civic and political life. For a time he was a Haven House leader, and he continues to remain active as a volunteer with Community Renewal. His story is like those of so many other young people today: breaking the cycle of poverty and hopelessness because of caring adults who show them a future full of hope.

Pam's Story

My friend Pam Morgan, now a community coordinator, is another Friendship House success story. In the mid 1990s, she had dropped out of school and was in an abusive relationship. She became addicted to drugs. Had she allowed herself to think about it, her life probably would have ended like those of so many low-income people in Shreveport at the time: overdose, murder, or early death due to poor health. Today, she describes herself at that period as "lost, without direction." Surviving day to day was hard enough with her three small children and a mother who was soon to die of cancer. The Friendship House changed her life.

It began in 2000 with an encounter with Annie "Jewel" Mariner, who was then our community coordinator in Allendale. Jewel, who lived in the Friendship House we built from scratch, initially went door to door just getting to know the people around her, cultivating purposeful friendship. Pam didn't know who this woman was and initially avoided her. She'd let the woman talk to her kids, but not to her directly. But, by Jewel's third visit Pam began to warm to Jewel's friendly advances. She sat on the front porch and talked to Jewel, whom she found warm and inviting.

Pam began sending her kids to the Friendship House Kids Club, a program designed to give the young people of the neighborhood a safe place to explore and grow together. It was not long before she could see that the program, and the Friendship House as a whole, was opening an entirely new direction in her family's life. It was a stark contrast to so much of her experience of Allendale up to that point. Unlike the houses that remained closed out of fear, the Friendship House was open, welcoming, and hopeful. Her experience there cracked open a space for her to develop some hope and soon led her to the difficult decision that she needed to stop using drugs. She was drawn to the positive attitudes she saw in Jewel and the others that worked at the Friendship House. They were real; they stayed. They helped kids with homework, taught them leadership skills, provided programs that let them know that they mattered.

In 2001, Pam began volunteering there, describing her family's daily routine as a rotation of home, school, and Friendship House. It was a place where her life had meaning, where she had something to give. She and her kids were the first ones there every day, and she loved doing whatever they asked. Jewel helped her to see a new way of thinking, of loving other people and serving people in need. She became a better mother to her children, and even began mothering other neighborhood children. She discovered she had much to give.

She began working there part time and eventually worked full time. It was not just her kids: she herself went through the Adult Renewal Academy and earned a high school diploma in 2012. She got a driver's license, and a car. She followed in Jewel's footsteps and became a community coordinator, purposefully reaching out to others in her neighborhood to support and encourage them and their children and grandchildren. In 2018, Pam moved into a second Friendship House that she herself had helped us build in Allendale. She now wants to make a difference in the lives of other women like her, and in the lives of the children in Allendale. And she does!

The New Settlement House Movement

Sometime after we had launched our Friendship House initiative, I picked up a book that had sat in my library for years, the autobiography of Jane Addams. The book is called *Twenty Years at*

Hull House. Published in 1893, I found it in a used bookstore and bought it due to a quotation that had been attributed to her, and which I always loved. She said, "The good we secure for ourselves is precarious and uncertain . . . until it is secured for all of us and incorporated into our common life."[6] It is a soul-igniting quote for me. But I knew nothing of Jane Addams or of Hull House. Providentially, I grabbed her book to read on vacation.

Have you ever heard of the settlement movement? I had not. Jane Addams was one of the leading lights. In fact, she was the first woman in the history of our country to win the Nobel Peace Prize (in 1931), and it was due to her work in the settlement movement. The life of this brilliant and committed woman is fascinating. But I must tell you of the settlement movement. First, the parched soil out of which it grew.

In the wake of the Industrial Revolution in the latter half of the nineteenth century, huge pockets of poverty were created in the Western nations. It is difficult to imagine living in the London of Dickens' *Oliver Twist.* The machine age began to spin out wasted humans through sweatshops, and sleaze oozed on the streets. Imagine seven-year-old girls working fifteen hours a day, six days a week and sometimes seven. All over Europe and America conditions spread that were dehumanizing at best.

But in London, in 1884, one Samuel A. Barnett, then vicar of St. Jude's Parish, invited a number of university students to join him and his wife in settling in the deprived and depraved area of east London. They believed that the only way to solve the problem of disintegration was to move into the neighborhood to live and to touch lives all around them, thus lifting broken people to

---

[6] Jane Addams, "The Subjective Necessity of Social Settlements," *Philanthropy and Social Progress* (New York: Thomas Y. Crowell, 1893), 7.

a new level of living and restoring their dignity embedded in a new destiny. It was wildly successful. The settlement was named Toynbee Hall and became known worldwide.[7] In 1888, Jane Addams, then on leave from medical school, visited the settlement, and her life was changed forever.

She returned to the United States and with friends founded a large house on the west side of Chicago where immense poverty was the order of the day. She purchased the house, named it Hull House, and moved in to stay. All over the United States, as well as the industrial West, settlement houses were being established with the same remarkable results first seen at Toynbee Hall. Lives were changed. Caring infrastructure was restored. And the capacity of the people to help themselves was wondrously renewed. The key was found.

The key ingredient to this success was dedicated people living with those whom they served. It worked one hundred years ago! It worked so well that the settlement houses could not contain all of the exploding programs. So they built community centers to run the overflow. Every community center built in America came out of the settlement movement. Neighborhoods were rebuilt from the inside out with astonishing success.

But what has happened? As best as I can see, they started relying on the buildings and programs of the community centers and stopped relying on the key ingredient of the settlers. *It is the settlers themselves loving their neighbors who bring the key dynamic of change and restoration necessary for renewal.* Being loved and loving others forever changes us. We should know that no mission succeeds without the missionaries.

---

[7] Toynbee Hall was named after fellow social reformer and friend of the Barnetts, Arnold Toynbee, who was the uncle of Arnold J. Toynbee, who authored *A Study of History* mentioned in Chapter 1 of this book.

Years after we began Friendship Houses, I discovered the historic roots from which the idea has grown and blossomed. The idea and the method are not new. We are simply recapturing something that we now know works. We have historical proof that the principles of empowering families to serve their neighbors works wildly well. Our model has an important difference, though: the families that move in already have roots in the community. They build and nurture the relationships that remake the community from the inside out. The same process happens in both gated communities and impoverished ones: neighbors reach out to neighbors, rebuilding the caring foundation of the neighborhood and allowing it to grow and thrive.

But I will add that we have also learned as we have moved along in this work. In the past each settlement house was both independent and self-sufficient. We have, since then, standardized the method and centralized the operation of the settlement movement, bringing a powerful unity to loving service, and this social technology will cultivate the growth of better persons and communities.[8]

---

[8] See Howard Husock, "Bringing Back the Settlement House," *Public Interest* 109 (Fall 1992), 53–72. Husock provides a logic that aligns with what our Friendship Houses are doing today.

5

Becoming Better Persons

The development of our social technology, relying on the three ingredients of Renewal Team, Haven House, and Friendship House, yielded countless stories of transformations of individuals and neighborhoods. To the names I have already mentioned, such as Tommy, Isaiah, Paige, Michael, Pam, and Robert, I could add hundreds and hundreds of others. As Shreveport Community Renewal grew to eventually become Community Renewal International (CRI)—becoming planted in other cities and even halfway across the world, in Cameroon—it became necessary to develop a more precise understanding of what kinds of persons we understood formed healthy communities. This understanding guides the way we discern how to dedicate time and resources to remaking our world.

We define a better person as a whole person. A whole person is both competent and compassionate. Those are the fundamentals that make a person whole. So what do we mean by competent? Competent persons have the willingness and the ability, within their highest capacity, to access and to appropriate resources within and outside of themselves that enable them to grow. And compassionate? Compassionate persons seek the good of others as they do their own. Whole persons are those who are on the predominant life trail of growing as well as caring. We say "predominant" because it indicates the fundamental direction of our lives. We are not always growing and caring, because we must allow for that most nagging of all human traits: failure. We slip, sometimes by accident, and unfortunately, sometimes by an act of will. But recovery and the important concept of repentance help us to set our faces to the sun again.

Six Basic Manifestations of Growing as a Human Being

1. We have the capacity to grow spiritually.

Because we are dealing with what are rock-bottom elements to growth, what we mean by spiritual growth always begins with the recognition that there is more to life than me, myself, and I. When I as a human being become aware that I am alive to do more than just conjugate the verb "to eat," and I choose to accept and enter into life with others, then I have begun the process of spiritual growth. I have recognized that there exists a reality that transcends me and that I am not the center of this universe. Note that I was careful to say "a reality" without explicating the nature of that reality. And note that I said "begins" with the recognition that there is more to life than me, myself, and I. All spiritual growth, as well as all other manifestations of growing, have so many dimensions that truly the sky is the limit. I should say spiritual growth is limitless, because the nature of our lives is such that growing itself has the possibilities of infinity.

The important point is that spiritual growth must be free. It cannot be forced. As members of the Renewal Team, our goal as individuals and organizations is to provide the network of care that is the nourishing soil of spiritual growth. Michael's word *positivity* is helpful here, too; people who work together to care for their neighbors help them to imagine a world where positive growth as persons is possible.

2. We can grow socially.

As life progresses, we all know that we must learn to get along not only with others, but also with ourselves. One of the greatest tragedies of human life and potential is the deadly phenomenon known as arrested development. Children are wonderful, but they are also childish. They are childish because they are children. To impose adult standards of behavior on children and demand their adherence is abuse. But to allow immature behavior to dictate development into maturity is deeply unfortunate. So we must grow in our relationships with our fellows and, again, with ourselves.

In the neighborhoods where we build Friendship Houses, we build one for children and another for teens and adults. We want there to be dedicated space where children can be children and learn the social skills that enable both self-knowledge and knowledge of how to play well with others. The Kids Clubs at the various Friendship Houses offer kids both fun and learning opportunities, such as field trips to parts of the city and parts of the country they might otherwise never experience. Our Girl Pearls, sponsored by a local sorority, helps girls with self-esteem building activities and career guidance. Perhaps most fundamentally, our community coordinators become the connective tissue that hold neighborhoods together, so that social bonds can grow over time and reestablish a foundation of caring.

One of the saddest things I have ever seen was scratched into the wooden door of the boys' bathroom in my elementary school. It was dug so deep that even after being painted over it was still legible. It was the message of some grade school kid. And it read, "I hate myself." I saw it every day and wondered who wrote it. I had not thought of that for many years, and only as I write these words did that memory return. After serving for years as a physician of the soul, and seeing the sorrow in so many wounded human beings, I only wonder why I haven't seen more scratched cries on the door eaves. Social growth always includes ourselves, because we are an integral part of any relationship with others. And in our Friendship Houses we have years of experience seeing young people who are given the chance to come to renewed self-understanding, so that they might enter relationships with others in a way that is life-giving and hopeful.

3. We can grow skillfully to navigate the tasks and opportunities presented by a complex world.

How important are life skills to meet both the small as well as the shattering demands that life imposes upon us? We can measure the crucial nature of this manner of growing by simply listing the books, videos, sermons, and proffered methods of how to deal with living in this world. Learning to navigate through life's unfolding journey, learning to respond situationally as challenges are dropped at our feet, and learning to appropriate the resources of our collective human experience, all equip us with skills not just to endure but to thrive.

The challenge in so many of our poor communities is that there is little access to skill building. Among the activities in Friendship Houses are many that offer exactly that: cooking classes, workout sessions, literacy classes, job preparation, and others. Children and adults have the opportunities to set and achieve goals, growing in confidence and self-understanding all along the way.

4. *We can grow intellectually.*

I am reminded of a cartoon I once saw in *The New Yorker* magazine. It showed two old codgers seated on a park bench feeding the squirrels. One of them reflected: "You know, I've learned a lot in these last eighty-five years. Unfortunately, most of it has been about aluminum." It made me laugh, but it can't possibly be true, for anyone. There is no graduation diploma from the school of life, but there ought to be. The great adventure of living must always include answering the high imperative of learning. To be captured by the wonder of the universe and to eagerly greet each day as another opportunity to participate in the majesty of meaning and discovery is enough to make Ponce de Leon's quest for the fountain of youth pale by comparison.

Some of the best stories that have emerged from our Friendship Houses in recent years are of boys and girls, men and women who achieve academic distinctions or scholarships through our afterschool programs or our Adult Renewal Academy. Operation H.O.P.E. (Helping Our Pupils Excel) is one example, giving students in grades six to twelve opportunities to learn and to make the transition from school to the workplace. The Adult Renewal Academy (ARA) is another, providing adults opportunities right in their own neighborhoods to earn their high school diploma and chart new paths to employment. My friend Gloria Millinder, whom I met just months into my return to Shreveport and who was one of the first five trustees of

Community Renewal, still oversees the ARA and loves quoting its motto: "We are walking up a driveway in our neighborhood that becomes a highway to a new life." She has helped scores of men and women over the years achieve a new life. She recently shared with me a representative story from one of them, a young man who has a diagnosed mental disability and who has served jail time. He wrote, "I don't think the world understands how much it means for a young Black man to be judged according to his past all his life by so many. And then the feeling he gets from finally being accepted. . . . The ARA staff truly believes in encouraging people, caring for people, and helping to change people's lives."

5. A whole person is always growing emotionally.

We grow emotionally as we channel our feelings, reactions, and impulses into positive and creative ways for ourselves and everyone around us. That is why compassion (feeling with) is the partner of competence in the nature of becoming a whole person. This imperative is so closely bound with social growth that it appears to be two sides of the same coin. Our emotional development is the critical energy that propels us in our relationships. We have been given a spectrum of emotions that can literally drive us crazy if they rule us, or on the other hand, can guide us to higher living if they are rightfully utilized. The old saying, "A fire in the curtains will burn your house down, but a fire in the oven will cook your meal," is sage advice. Our emotions can be a whole howling zoo when allowed to dictate our day. And there is nothing more fickle than feelings. How do you feel now? Well, if you don't like it, then wait just a minute and it will change. Growing emotionally never means the denial of feelings or their suppression or even their unguarded expression.

It is difficult to quantify the way that our social technology helps people to grow emotionally. Yet if you talk to the people who participate in our programs, one thing becomes abundantly clear: they are happy to be part of them. Happiness, of course, is more than an emotion, but happy people can often tell the difference between their past emotional experiences and their present ones. The key difference for people who commit themselves to caring is that they deepen their capacity "to feel with others" (the definition of *compassion*). Our Renewal Team is composed of people who are growing emotionally because they are part of a community of growth.

6. *Finally, we grow physically.*

I used to love it when my uncle would come to visit when I was a child. He had the gift of affirming the most exciting thing about childhood: I was growing. "My gosh," he would bellow, "you've gotten a whole head taller since I saw you last. Man, you've grown." Today, the very last word that I want to hear from anyone, especially my family and my visiting friends who have not laid eyes on me for a while, are the words, "Man, you've grown." But physical growth is vital. We should stop growing big and continue to grow in healthful ways. Like it or not, we are grounded in our bodies. And if I have a toothache, I promise you that I am not thinking of ways to express my compassion toward others or of the other ways I can grow. Our body, if we can manage it, should be so finely tuned that we don't even notice that it's running. As human beings, we certainly cannot avoid sickness or tragic and painful physical circumstances. But we can avoid choices that deliberately afflict us with their diminishing consequences.

It is important not to lose sight of this manifestation of growing, particularly among young people who may not have access to safe parks or nutritious food. Because we have developed a system of caring, children in our Friendship House programs have a healthy meal and a network of adults who foster in them habits of wellness. In a later chapter I'll describe the way CRI is rebuilding the ever-renewing village, and how one of the exciting areas of growth is our partnership with a major health care provider in Shreveport who will work with us to address the social determinants of health—those factors in a society that can impede people's ability to achieve wellness. If we address people's physical needs, then the other manifestations of growth are more likely to unfold as well.

Summing Up:
Competent and Compassionate

A whole person is both competent and compassionate. We said that compassionate means to seek the good of others as we do our own. Over the last few years amazing discoveries within the physiological makeup of human beings have revealed the existence of the biological basis for compassion—for "feeling with" others. Scientists tell us that mirror neurons are embedded in our brains that enable us to have the capacity to feel with other creatures.[1] Have you ever wondered why you smile back at a

---

[1] Mirror neurons were discovered in monkeys by chance in 1992. Scientists continue to probe how these neurons function when human beings imitate one another. See Cecilia Heyes and Caroline Catmur, "What Happened to Mirror Neurons?" *Perspectives on Psychological Science* 17, no. 1 (January 2022): 153–68. https://doi.org/10.1177/1745691621990638.

person who smiles at you? It is not just courtesy; it is reflex. You have to concentrate not to smile. The ancients would not have been surprised at all by this discovery within our brains. The wisest among them always rose to the top of the ethical tree by teaching that our best behavior comes when we can so identify with the feelings and circumstances of others that we embrace them just as if their experiences were happening to us.

Empathy is the term we use to describe this capacity within us. It is a precious gift that can be cultivated through conscious practice and exercise. But note that our capacity to feel what others are feeling issues forth from the throne of our own feelings. Here we see that we are so in tune with ourselves that we project how we approach and interact with others just as we would like to be so treated. How incredibly wise!

Whole philosophical schools were founded upon the notion that we must come to grips with what makes us *sui generis*—unique—an unrepeated and unrepeatable miracle. Think of humankind's wrestling in this long journey with our selves. First, Socrates said the solution was to know thyself, because the unexamined life is not worth living.[2] But if I made that path my sole highway, I would be like the monkey chasing the weasel round and round the mulberry bush to find "me." Next, Epicurus said that the best way to find yourself is to express yourself.[3] And while both suppression and repression are deadly poisons when taken in excess, they are necessary to cage the tangle of desires arising from an insatiable self inside us. The pleasure principle shows the law of diminishing returns even as we make higher and higher investment. So the Stoics came along and countered

---

[2] Plato, *Apology*, line 37e.
[3] See "Epicurus' Letter to Menoeceus," in Diogenes Laertius, *Lives of Eminent Philosophers*, book 10.

that we must control ourselves.[4] All of us know that self-control is vital. But it is also ultimately defeating when it is made the primary means of life. What energy we must spend keeping the selfish beast within caged! Jailbreaks happen regularly. Finally, there is a school that says, give yourself.[5] Jesus, of course. It is in seeking another's well-being just as we seek our own that the force of feelings is channeled and flows to wholeness.

Think for a moment of the profound implications of this. The old adage "the meek shall inherit the earth" (Mt 5:5; Ps 37:11) now makes sense, because it refers to a person who is, to use an adjective of the Greek philosophers, *praus*, referring to a powerful but bridled horse. Therefore, it is not the namby-pamby fragile passive dewdrops that will win this world. It will be those who are trained and disciplined. It is our very powerful and trained selves. Every soldier surrenders self for a cause outside of self. And if that cause is the highest cause of seeking the good of others as we seek our own good, then we will win. A trained army beats an untrained army every single time.

A whole person is both competent and compassionate. We were now on our way with a workable understanding of what kind of person would be needed to fill our societies in order to ever renew the world of human beings. But then we ran straight into the Gordian knot of devising a system that produces whole persons. The struggle with the all-critical "how" had now commenced. A critical truth began to be realized and consciously examined. Human beings cannot grow or care without others. That seems so incredibly simple. But think of this truth, we all

---

[4] See especially Epictetus, *Enchiridion*.

[5] See, for example, Matthew 20:28: "The Son of Man came not to be served but to serve."

must choose for ourselves to grow and to care. No one can do this for us.

There is simply no proxy for becoming whole persons. Yet, *although we must make these choices alone, we cannot fulfill them without others.* No one grows in isolation. The very fact that you are reading these words means that your capacity has been enabled by a world of human beings. Even if we choose to denounce and withdraw from society, saying, "I have no need of you," the very fact of our existence sets the lie to that fallacy. No one is an island.

It is here that the primacy of relationships is revealed as the vital core of life. The central urge for all of us moves us inexorably to seek self-fulfillment. Unlike my pet dog, I want to be better. I have the capacity to see what I could be and what I should be. Then I look in the mirror and see what I am, and I know that there is a yawning gulf separating what I am from what I could or should be. And all of my seeking lies in finding a way to become what I could and certainly should be. This existential gap is the source of both fulfillment and frustration. It is how we are made.

"The Lord God said, 'It is not good that man should be alone'" (Gen 2:18). But the beauty of this longing lies in the fact that it drives us to enter the world of relationships seeking fulfillment with one another. And please see that I didn't write *from* one another. This is because the temptation ever lurking in the world of relationships is to use another to satiate the desire to fill the gaps of our lives. This is the fundamental meaning of lust. Lust is to use another human being as an object, or a means, or an "it" for one's own gratification. It is sexual, to be sure, but lust is vastly more than that. It can stretch across the whole gamut of our interactions. The irony, as Martin Buber has taught us, is that when we use another as an "it," action becomes like a noiseless file sawing away something essential in us, and we are in peril of becoming diminished ourselves.[6] So how we relate within our relationships can grow us or shrink us. We become how we treat others.

As I wrote in the beginning of this chapter, only positive relationships grounded in compassion can ultimately produce the kind of human beings needed to renew our lives and societies. When we begin to develop friendships and then consciously choose to commit to those positive relationships, we find an amazing world. This is the world where unlimited growth can and does occur.

Endless Growth

If we think about it, everything around us will decay. Decay is everywhere. Our earth, we are told, has approximately five billion years before our sun will go nova and put an end to our planet. Nothing lasts forever. Several years ago, during a move, I ran across my long-lost high school yearbooks. When we open our yearbook, we don't just turn the page automatically to see our teachers. First, we look at our own picture. So, following personality protocol, I went to my picture. What a colossal mistake! Here on the verge of my fiftieth high school reunion, I discovered to my horror that I was the poster child of decay. Decay! I am reminded of the story of a rather a distraught woman who approached a famous astrophysicist following his lecture on the universe and almost breathlessly asked, "Professor, did you say the universe would end in a trillion years or a trillion trillion years?"

---

[6] Martin Buber, *I and Thou*, trans. Walter Kaufman (New York: Touchstone, 1971).

"Madam, I said a trillion trillion years." "Oh," she exclaimed, "that's a relief."

Still, decay is not the whole story. There is another reality in which the opposite is true. This is the reality that lives within positive and caring relationships. Within the world of positive relationships lies the possibility of endless growth. Think of this. We can never know all there is to know about ourselves. Neither can our friends ever know all about us. That is because the human personality is so large and so dynamic that we can spend a lifetime simply exploring and discovering one another, never exhausting the yet-unseen worlds within.

So as we continue to intentionally commit to our friendships and consciously give ourselves to them, we actually grow closer and closer and closer, with no end in sight, because we can never know all there is to know about one another. That is why the greatest adventure in life, one that brings both surprise and joy while at the same time bringing security and comfort, is the adventure of friendship. Everything I know decays—except positive relationships, best illustrated by true friendship. Positive relationships, when we seek them, dwell in them, and make them the goal of life, show us that we can inhabit a world that gets better and better and better. I sometimes have wet-behind-the-ears young fellows ask me, when finding out that my loving mate and I have been together for half a century, "Do you ever get tired of kissing your wife?" My answer is simple and quick: "Heck no. It just gets better and better and better. There are years upon years piled up in every kiss."

It is a mistake to think that this world is one of straight-line progress driving deep and high all of the time forever. Of course it is not. Positive relationships have fits and starts, failures and faults to the maximum. But even those things which we accurately count as negatives within our friendships can actually be utilized to feed a growing closeness. There are always two fundamental stages to positive relationships. The first is the decision to start the friendship, and the second, based on conscious commitment renewed until it is unconsciously applied, is the decision to remain friends. Some call these stages the attraction stage and the attachment stage. The economy and ecology of positive relationships are truly something to behold.

Nothing is wasted when commitment to a friendship becomes the guiding imperative. As we mess up in small or even in big ways with each other, those violations are transformed into growth when we follow the simple rules guiding the universe of positive relationships. We must admit to our friend, "my bad." We must sincerely commit to becoming better in the future to ourselves and our friend. And our friend must forgive us. Forgiveness is the restoration of a relationship bruised or broken by our "bad." It means also releasing the hurt, knowing that sometimes this does take time.

Please note that I used the word *must* over and over. I want us to be reminded that this universe of positive relationships is governed by laws that are just as inflexible and immutable as the laws of our physical universe. And every true law (whether known or unknown) dealing with the reality of our existence has consequences if it is either fulfilled or violated.

As we enter and abide in the universe of positive relationships based on decisions and actions, not only are we living in the reality of an ever-growing, ever-renewing, ever-progressing world with one another, but we discover another magnificent truth. As our friendships grow in quality and quantity, we grow toward wholeness as persons. So now we have one part of the answer to growing a world that gets better and better and better without an end in sight. We can grow better people through positive relationships.

A human being grows to wholeness only within positive relationships. If we recall the image of the swimming-pool filter, the whole person is the atom and friendships are the molecules making up all of society. If we do not understand that, and start there, we will fail. But we have billions of human atoms and millions of human molecules that we must address all at once or we will fail. And it became clear to us that we must take this truth and enfold it into a system that would deal with every atom/molecule and the whole pool all at the same time. It was *Eureka!* time for us. We discovered that we did not have to dream up or invent a system that provided a way to grow human beings in wholeness and at the same time address whole groups. Approximately fourteen thousand years ago a system was developed that utterly transformed the entire human race. We call it the village. And we can recover its genius.

6

"Re-village-izing" Society

Much has been written through the years about the amazing invention of the village. And we have learned a great deal about the power and the dynamism that village life have contributed to the human journey. The village can rightly lay claim to being the longest-lasting collective dwelling of human beings in our entire history. Its nature, structure, and significance gave us the perfect paradigm for engaging the whole of society itself.

Village to City, Back to Village

While the village has been the vehicle for transforming the human race from isolated clusters of humans into social beings appropriating tremendous scope and power, it, too, is limiting when taking into account the entire spectrum of our nature and potential. There is a reason that we are leaving the village as we know it. And there is a reason that the village was historically overgrown with towns, then cities, and then nations. So one answer for the eclipsing of the village is this simple logic: if a village is good, then a bigger village is better.

This totally understandable progression fits our nature perfectly. If one slice of pizza is good, then just try to prevent me from eating more! Growth continued unabated from villages to hamlets to towns into great cities and then city-states until the village disappeared. But just as we discover that what was good with one slice of pizza may not be so good if we ate the whole extra-large triple-topping double-cheese pie, so unbounded city growth lost the nurturing and nourishing function so necessary to secure and launch our effective means of producing an environment for growing whole human beings. The common value—desiring better environments for human dwelling—is one reason why we left the village. It is obvious that city life does meet some of our needs. But it is also clear that we gave up something to gain something. And there are other reasons for leaving the village as we know it.

The nurturing and nourishing nature of the village is absolutely crucial to human development in our drive and quest for wholeness, and our basic hungering and thirsting need for the belonging and tending quality of the village is absolutely real. But there is still an indefinable desire in human beings to venture forth into new lands. History has confirmed that the human race is always journeying on to worlds beyond. In so many ways our village home was confining in its familiar and conserving cycles of group living. Just as we crave routine and its security, we also are made to search for the new thrill of adventure.

Add to this almost instinctual desire to seek the new and the better the power of human relational interaction to grow us and inspire us, and we have found another reason why the nurturing arms of the village were not enough to meet all our needs. A genius within a village would have probably been dubbed the village idiot, given that person's clear development as someone oddly different. But within a much larger community the chance of more geniuses was surely possible. Here their interaction could produce thinking that, while mocked in the beginning, proved to have lifting power by and for all. The ancient proverb,

"As iron sharpens iron, so one person sharpens another," has the ring of truth.

The discovery that differentiation and variety breeds creativity in ways impossible for homogeneity to produce was a seminal insight in the history of the development of our human race. Then came the realization that cross-cultural connections had the capacity to grow whole social groups. This historical "*aha!*" developed over eons and began to move us exponentially in cultural growth. We could add a whole multitude of need- and desire-satisfying reasons for leaving our villages. In the scope of history the human race reached out to grasp the brass ring of growth that went beyond the village.

Still, our societal mother remains the village. It was there that the trajectory of our entire journey in growth was formed, and birthed, nourished and nurtured, and finally launched. Lewis Mumford was absolutely right when he declared the invention of the village to be one of the great transformational moments of the human race.[1] So let us continue to study that wonderful phenomenon that fed us individually and led us collectively all at one and the same time.

It is possible to reclaim the virtues of the village, which would move us into a step-by-step, systematic approach to engage effectively whole cities of whatever size. The old African adage, "How do you eat an elephant? You do it bite by bite," sheds wisdom for every daunting task. The life of the village nourished and replicated over and over in every city could literally reconnect all of us into a powerful transformational force of ever-renewing relationships.

---

[1] Lewis Mumford, "The Natural History of Urbanization," in *Man's Role in Changing the Face of the Earth*, ed. William L. Thomas Jr. (Chicago: University of Chicago Press, 1956).

Eight Elements of the Village

Even as the body flows together and works together as one unified organism, one can easily discern its major parts. This is also true with the life of the village. We identified eight fundamental elements making up a village in order to have intelligible handles for our leavening tactics in restoring a working system of relationships today:

1. A safe and secure environment
2. Common values
3. Adequate dwellings
4. Meaningful work
5. A healthcare delivery system
6. A means of education
7. Leadership
8. Mutually enhancing relationships (we'll end up giving this last one a chapter all its own).

These elements make up the whole body of the village. They are fundamental to its existence and daily life. And while in the dynamism of living they flow together seamlessly to produce this marvel of social structure, they can be compartmentalized for the sake of addressing the whole.

René Descartes was a great seventeeth-century French philosopher and thinker whose approach to problem solving has had a massive influence on Western civilization. What we came to call Cartesian categorizing, flowing from the spring of Aristotle, always compartmentalized the elements of any body of thought in order to comprehend and therefore rationally approach them. This is a great method of understanding, but it has led us also to separate elements from the whole as we seek to solve the individual component challenges. And then we realize that we are stumped in putting Humpty Dumpty back together again in any meaningful way.

This analytical approach has been our entire method to solving the problem of poverty in America. We can dissect a frog and learn about its atoms, molecules, tissues, and organs, but we kill it in the process. The pioneering systems thinker Donella H. Meadows points out that when we propound the truth that two and two equals four, we show that we have diligently studied the two and we have studied the equals and we have studied the four. But only now are we beginning to study the "and."[2] I like to think that while we have embraced Descartes' famous dictum, "I think therefore I am," that we would also bond that individual truth to the social truth of the African proverb, "Because we are, I am." We must always be mindful of the whole when we undertake the study of its parts.

When two or more human hearts truly work together (what psychologist Abraham Maslow called "peak experience"[3]), more than harmony is created. What is created is an entirely new entity. We have captured this truth in the German word *gestalt* to point to the wholeness of an existing form. We have to grasp this wholeness if we are to approach our world with even a modicum of accuracy. Whether we are speaking of individuals, the societies in which we live, or the global village, seeking to grasp the whole means thinking beyond our individual needs and desires.

The English word *synergy* comes from the Greek *synergo*, "to work together," and refers to the interaction of many component parts to produce a whole that is greater than the sum of those parts. Think of yourself. You are more than your looks, body, mind, and will. You are more than where you came from, your

---

[2] Donella H. Meadows, citing an ancient Sufi teaching, in *Thinking in Systems: A Primer* (London: Earthscan, 2009), 12.

[3] Abraham H. Maslow, *Religions, Values, and Peak Experiences* (Columbus: Ohio State University Press, 1964).

race, nationality, and all of the other "yours" pertinent to you. But you are not divorced from each and all either. You are always more than the sum of each. And when two of us come together to truly share, there is more than just the two of us. In essence we combine our individual "more" with another's "more" in greater or lesser ways and a new "more" is created that transcends both.

We are all aware of this elusive phenomenon of human interaction because we feel it at various times and in different settings. Take team spirit, for instance. It is always great to be a winning team, but you can have a winning team and still not have team spirit. On the contrary, you can lose every game and still have that incredible sense of bonding that comes with team spirit. Think of the various ways that we human beings have in gathering together and also the experiences when all of us *felt* that there was something more present that bonded us in real but inexpressible ways.

In the same way, note the reality of another new presence when two people fall in love. When two people enter that peak experience, they know it. They simply cannot express all that it is. Songs have been sung, poems have been written, and every manner of expression known to all of us cannot wrap up with a ribbon and a pretty package all that we *feel*. When we come together for a shared purpose, a new reality is created that is greater than each and all of us put together. Yet each is nourished. So in identifying the component parts of the village, we always remember that each is inextricably bound to the others and all flow together.

As we delineated the basics of the village, we went all the way back to its beginnings in order to understand the fundamentals of its structural life. The eight fundamental elements listed above gave us the universal description for those fundamentals. Please see that some of the essentials taught in urban planning are missing, such as the vital element of transportation. The same is true with communication or any other means of coming together. When the village was formed, there were certain things that were human that we counted as given. Fourteen thousand years ago the only mode of transportation rested upon human legs. If you were human and healthy, you could walk. So we just assume that is part of the package and not a special element of the village of human beings. There were domesticated dogs by then, but they would be hard for adults to ride. Cattle were domesticated about ten thousand years ago; horses were tamed about six thousand years ago; and the earliest wheels were invented around five thousand years ago. But the village existed for thousands of years before the technology of transportation was added.

A Safe and Secure Environment

The villager fundamentally must be secure and safe. This element is vital because there can never be bonding without feeling secure enough to come together. And that gathering, by virtue of increasing numbers and the specialization of tasks strengthening the group, increased both safety and security exponentially. It is important to note that safety is an environmental reality and security is a psychological perception, a state of mind. For instance, a person could be perfectly safe living in a guarded and gated community in many an American city and still feel scared to death. The environment is safe, but the person's mind has snakes in it. On the other hand, a person could be living in a truly dangerous environment, know it, but still feel secure and calm within themselves going about their business.

I might add, parenthetically, that the notion that gated communities are both safe and community enhancing is often fallacious. They are neither safe nor community enhancing in times of declining civilization. Over and over throughout history the answer for more advanced (or even wealthier) people to protect themselves from those they deemed barbarians (or in other words, anyone who is not "us") was to both distance and run up a wall with a gate for protection. This answer has neither checked the advance of decline nor protected the besieged. So ultimate safety in real or perceived advance of the barbarians is a fiction. All we have to do is remember the walls of Jericho, or long before that just think of Troy.

If conditions of real or perceived deprivation continue unhealed, then eventually those who have fled to "safety" behind the barricades will be swallowed in the tide of disintegrating culture. If our cities continue to disintegrate, then no one is safe. A gated community may bring safety for a generation in a declining situation. But as disintegration proceeds and danger becomes acute, how do our gated inhabitants function? Do they have their groceries airlifted? Go to work in a desert? Fleeing is not an effective method of combating cultural disintegration. It only delays the inevitable.

About ten miles outside of Paris, France, the premier gated community of the modern era was on display: Versailles. It was a world apart from the suffering and the squalor of the majority of Parisians. Nothing could have been safer. It was the home of a king who ruled by Divine Right. But, on October 5, 1789, after years and years of deprivation, smoldering anger exploded into fury, first with the women working the docks gutting and scaling fish with their long sharp knives, and then with a gathering mob of thousands. They marched the ten miles to Versailles, stormed the gates, decapitated many of the royal guard, parading their heads on pikes, and then burst upon the palace itself. They ran up the stairs seeking to kill the queen and everyone else in their way. Marie Antoinette escaped her room by a whisker and took refuge, running down the hall to the king's chambers. The fisherwomen, missing her, instead attacked her room, cut her mattresses to shreds, and slashed her clothes into ribbons. The mob then held the royal family hostage, eventually parading them in their carriage back to Paris where at the age of thirty-eight, January 21, 1793, Louis the Sixteenth was beheaded. Nine months later, at the same age, his wife, Marie Antoinette, also was beheaded.

I share these rather stark reminders to underscore the fact that gated communities in declining conditions are only a temporary reprieve. That strategy will not stop the encroaching process of decline. Gated communities are not ultimately safe, regardless of the developer's promises or residents' hopes. Not only do gated communities fail to provide true safety in sick social times, but they also do not provide the one cure for that sickness. As a matter of fact, they inadvertently contribute to the conditions by which the malaise can spread. The separate and oasis-quality life behind walls may assuredly provide a bonding experience for the inhabitants within those walls, but the walls themselves limit the power of that community to transform the conditions around it that ultimately, if not transformed, will devour.

The key is to address the entire pool. Regaining village values must be done without walls and gates.

Furthermore, our task is to make the desert bloom, not to build an oasis. Even if we were able to overcome our tendency to put our trust in gated communities as the solution to community renewal, we must build into such a plan, as an imperative, that once we have achieved specified conditions of safety, then the walls would come down. And that must be rigorously adhered to, because our human tendency is to keep the walls up rather than the counterintuitive but true fact that only when the walls are removed can we gain true security, and therefore true safety, in a consciously ever-caring community that we work to nourish each and every day.

Please understand that I am not seeking to impugn the motives of people who live in gated communities. They are not bad or uncaring human beings any more than people who live in impoverished conditions are the opposite. Just as there are some mighty mean folks who live in mansions, some of the most wonderful people I know also live in mansions. And just as there are some of the most transformational human beings I know who live in honest-to-goodness shanties, some mighty mean folks dwell there, too.

The motives behind the movement to gated communities are mixed, and there is a desire for safety and security that is pulling us into that strategy. But the point remains that this strategy will not achieve our ultimate hope of living with a safe and loving world.

Rome fell in 410 CE with the invasion of Alaric and the Visigoths. But in the years just prior, Honorius, the emperor, issued nine different imperial edicts forbidding the Roman patricians from leaving Rome and moving to their country villas. They were bailing out of the big walled city to their little walled villas to escape the rot within Rome itself. So even within walls, if we are not working to grow our community in caring for one another, we have a most miserable time because then we are with folks on the inside that make us a mite uncomfortable, to say the least. Community life becomes untenable unless we are intentional in its fundamental nurture.

Renewal by its very nature, if it is real and living, cannot be contained. So community renewal is actually doing what it must do within these gated communities. It is flowing out of the gates and over the walls and reaching to everyone around. As that tide continues, and I have no doubt that it will, given the incredible commitment of the residents and their leaders to a new community for our world, we will eventually see the gates disappear and the walls fall down. As Robert Frost reminds us in his 1914 poem "Mending Walls": "Something there is that doesn't love a wall / that wants it down."

Common Values

Add to safety and security another fundamental of the village: common values. The more life values we share in common, the more ways we are able to cement our connections with one another. But the critical truth here is that no connections are possible without the shared commitment to something in common that transcends us. So a village of human beings is a village because its inhabitants are communalized around shared values usually derived from a fundamental value. Sociologists tell us that our behavior flows from and to our commonly held values. We learn generationally the things that we must do and the things that we must not do in order to live within and be a part of the community of the village. Thus the communal rules that we enact that lead to the edification of the village grow us within the highest value of our community. We cannot ultimately grow alone or in a social vacuum.

Remember that whole persons are competent human beings who have the willingness and the ability to access and to appropriate, within their highest potential, resources within and outside of themselves that enable them to grow. Understanding how we grow is of critical importance if we are consistently to create the social conditions necessary to grow to wholeness. We must be able to access and to appropriate all of the inner resources that enable us to persevere and to grow through the living of our days. Those inner resources are largely instilled through our social interactions. Add to our basic temperament the learned overlay of generations of life coping, and we have our wellsprings of inner resources.

Of utmost importance for individual growth is the willingness and ability to access and appropriate the resources outside ourselves. You and I are limited in our individual capacities merely by being human. If we truly want to grow, then we must be willing to grow, and we all know the difference. I may want to be slim and fit, but I am just not willing to give up candy bars and comfort. To be willing means that I must consciously take steps that bring me under a discipline. In effect, I surrender myself to the process that I perceive will bring about the desired result.

In order to grow in maturity and wholeness, we must be willing to give ourselves to the values that transcend us individually, because the social values have the capacity to carry us down the road in our quest for individual growth. I can swim, but I am not the best swimmer in the world. But even if I were the greatest swimmer in the world, I could not swim from California to Hawaii. But this limitation does not mean that we are incapable of getting to Hawaii as human beings. We are able to appropriate a vehicle that has the capacity to take us there.

We must choose a vehicle that can take us there. We can choose to drift by trade winds on a raft without a sail. We can choose to appropriate the power of the wind in a sailboat. We can motorize the boat. We can join a cruise ship for a luxurious passage. Or we can choose a luxury jet airliner. Traveling to our destination bullet fast and sipping lemonade does have its appeal.

But before we can appropriate this power to take us to the fulfillment of our desired goal, we must give ourselves to a discipline that enables us to be successful. We must limit some of our freedoms for a season in order to arrive at our desired point. We must choose to proceed to enter a confined arena. So I voluntarily give up spatial movement even to the extent that I must remain in my seat at the command of the pilots, whose experienced wisdom I must trust. The parallel is this: An entire society makes and keeps possible the reality of the plane and its efficiency itself. Think of the variegated airline industry all working to provide your fast, safe, and comfortable flight. We are totally dependent upon the years of advance in airplane development, as well as the effective maintenance and guidance of each craft. By giving ourselves to the passenger role, we benefit by societal cooperation in achieving our dream destination.

Consider the common values of the village. *Common values are the social vehicle that have the possibility of enabling unlimited individual growth in becoming a whole person.* We cannot go far on our own in this journey of life with our knapsack labeled, "Made by Me." Some values are like rafts, and some are like luxury jet airliners. What can be adjudged by the collective wisdom of the human race as the highest of values is so considered because it has been seen as the value that has the greatest capacity to grow both individual persons and therefore their societies, thereby actualizing their maximum potential in seeking one another's good.

Some previously held common values have proven not to be the best vehicle for ultimate human growth. For instance, take a village whose inhabitants practiced cannibalism. That practice was a common value, and while the villagers were bonded by that common practice, thus deriving some social benefit to themselves by being a part of a community, it was, in hindsight, a vehicle that had severe limitations in taking them where they desired to go. It was a practice that certainly was not good for their neighboring villages. And when a better vehicle came along, then this value became obsolete. Folks finally realized that devouring others and risking being devoured is not the best way to seek the good of others as we do our own.

It is fascinating to watch the flow of growth in the history of our human race. Because it is really the growth of our discernment in common values that always moves out from self to others in increasingly larger and larger circles.

American poet Edwin Markham penned these words in "Outwitted" in 1915:

> He drew a circle that shut me out—
> Heretic, a rebel, a thing to flout.

> But Love and I had the wit to win:
> We drew a circle that took him in!

Markham was dead reckoning in the direction the human race must travel if we would be whole. It is important to note that we are not known for giving up our common values readily or willy-nilly. We will long hold onto values that continue to be proven rudimentary vehicles to wholeness, and halting in progress. But if those common values are all we see or have, then we will hold them in a societal death grip. How interesting to see, then, that we can let the old go. Common values can change when enough folks see that there is a better vehicle for taking us where we want to go.

In the early nineteenth century the great Thomas Chalmers totally captured this truth of value change in his famous sermon "The Expulsive Power of a New Affection."[4] Chalmers pegged what we all intuit, and that is the truth that we will not let a familiar habit or value go unless and until we can see something that we believe will serve us better. In this age of mass communications, the common values of different villages no longer grow in isolation from one another. As a human family we have the capacity to learn from one another if, like my story about the ants earlier, we are willing to learn what will make us all thrive.

Adequate Dwellings

Human beings have to have some form of protection from their environment. We live in something that brings us protection from the weather and terrestrial conditions around us, as rudimentary as a makeshift poncho or as resplendent as an ornate

---

[4] Thomas Chalmers, *The Expulsive Power of a New Affection* (London: Hatchers and Co., 1861).

palace. Our dwellings provide us with the possibility of tending to the need for solitude as well as sociality. The ebb and flow of our lives move dynamically from our need for time alone to a need for time together and back again. Our collective wisdom has shown that the dwellings of a village that allowed for this ebb and flow were of vital importance. It was within this fundamental village element that the building blocks of society were grown.

It is possible to imagine a world in which all people have adequate dwellings, and of the goods that would flow from such a world. The partnership that CRI has had with the Fuller Center for Housing, which I'll describe in Chapter 8, is evidence of the kind of transformation possible when a community prioritizes making adequate dwellings a real possibility for all residents. Dwellings cannot of themselves create a community, but it is impossible to imagine a real community in which some people do not have a place to live.

Meaningful Work

The most basic meaning of work is that activity which will provide for the sustenance of our physical need to survive. That is why I call it meaningful work. It has nothing to do with lofty philosophical constructs or deep psychological drives at all. The most primitive form of work gathers food for survival. And it is meaningful if enough food is gathered to live another day or two. It really does not mean much of anything for living if you can only find a bone a day. What that means is you simply are not going to make it for very long.

At the same time, meaningful work must occur, given the need to construct and repair our dwellings for adequacy in meeting our needs. And given the conditions of the climate, it was in most circumstances essential to gather fuel for the village fires and to fashion clothing for protection from sun or snow. The time would come when we continued to work more in order to begin to advance beyond surviving. We learned quickly that more efficient work as well as work together meant that we could begin to thrive. The village structure both absorbed that principle as well as exemplified it.

Today, our attitudes toward work are caught between the two extremes of excess and defect. On one hand is the phenomenon of burnout, the tendency to work to excess to the exclusion of nearly every other meaningful pursuit in life.[5] On the other hand is the painful reality of unemployment or underemployment, which afflicts many households. Neither of these extremes unfolds in isolation from other factors: cost of living, accessibility of childcare, health issues, and so many others. Both extremes represent forms of alienation. In the former case, that alienation is often characterized by the distance created by screens that separate people from the actual fruits of their labor or other people who help make the work light. Many live in the virtual rather than real world, which provides little human interaction to give life to one's work. In the latter case, the inability to attain meaningful work—whether because of one's social geography, illness, criminal record, or poor education—separates people from that which might lift them out of a cycle of poverty. The pandemic years have added new layers to these distinctions, and it remains to be seen how much meaningful work will be done across virtual divides of physical separations. What is needed is a reclaiming of a facet of work that we easily lose in a digital age: the reality that work is itself a social relation by which we knit together the fabric of a village.

---

[5] For an analysis of this tendency, see Jonathan Malesic, *The End of Burnout: Why Work Drains Us and How to Build Better Lives* (Berkeley and Los Angeles: University of California Press, 2022).

A Healthcare Delivery System

Every village had some kind of healthcare delivery. Whether it was a shaman using juju, or the stored knowledge of roots and herbs, our village forebears had ways to address the myriad ways that we fragile human beings could be physically afflicted. The need to see to the physical well-being of everyone became an early priority in group life and served to become a fundamental element in village life as well.

In 1923, Dr. Albert Schweitzer, who was awarded the Nobel Peace Prize in 1952, published a masterpiece. It was a two-volume work entitled *The Philosophy of Civilization*. In this profound study Schweitzer defined civilization not based upon the perfecting of gadgetry but upon the possessing of morality. He showed compellingly that the advancement of technology is not the accurate measure of whether or not a society is civilized. Rather, how we behave toward one another and all of the life on our globe, which is grounded in the height or depth of our morality, is the determining factor of our growth from primitive to civilized. This means that a society may have a stone-age technology but still be highly civilized based upon the empathy that reigns in its relationships. And the opposite could occur. We might be bathed and immersed in all kinds of fancy and futuristic gadgets, yet treat one another like tools to be used for our own gratification. Or we may treat our kind right but blister all others. In this case we are not advanced human beings, according to Schweitzer. We are uncivilized at our core. This incredible insight, ironically finished by Schweitzer while he and his family were being held in a French World War I detention camp, presciently described his native country's monstrous turn under Nazi rule. What better example than to see brilliant gadgetry used for horrific acts. This was primitive and not civilized.

Just think of the massive and brilliant technology that is serving humankind in this twenty-first century. I cannot imagine the multiple breakthroughs that are gaining our lives years if not decades of healthy living, even now as I write these words. It is simply staggering how we can diagnose, cure, and even prevent human illness. But I also see the simply unconscionable truth that some thirty million human beings in the United States have no healthcare delivery system assurance if they get sick.[6] And the greatest threat to health in our land is to be poor.

This is not civilized morality. It is primitive. But it is more than that. It is a betrayal of the highest morality we have been given as a human race. The words "as surely as you did it to one of the least of these" and "as surely as you did not do it to one of the least of these" (Mt 25:40, 45) call us to the best within us. When we measure our progress by how the least among us are progressing, then we measure our capacity for morality and our own notions of civilization. Perhaps it would help us to remember that the words above followed the words, "I was sick and you took care of me" (v. 36) and "I was sick and in prison and you did not visit me" (v. 43). Civilization is at its highest and best when it lives within us to see the least of us as us. The village had a healthcare delivery system because the villagers cared about the health of one another and saw it as essential to being a community.

A Means of Education

The village also had education as a crucial element in its life and existence. Education is the means by which both knowledge and wisdom are transmitted from one generation to another.

---

[6] National Health Interview Survey of the Centers for Disease Control and Prevention, February 2021. See Kenneth Finegold, Ann Conmy, Rose C. Chu, Arielle Bosworth, and Benjamin D. Sommers, "Trends in the US Uninsured Population, 2010–2020," https://aspe.hhs.gov/system/files/pdf/265041/trends-in-the-us-uninsured.pdf.

As the human race perseveres, the wealth of knowledge should become a vast storehouse that should feed the progression of wisdom. Knowledge comprises our grasping of facts, concepts, and methods. Wisdom has always been considered the right use of knowledge for individual benefit and societal betterment. T. S. Eliot, in his 1934 play *The Rock,* was right to ask, "Where is the wisdom we have lost in knowledge?"

Education in the village was a fundamental way in which the villagers were able to store knowledge and wisdom collectively in a powerful dynamic process. And before the invention of writing, the group memory was served through storytelling and the rites of passage for young people. At the heart of this process was the apprenticeship method of acquiring knowledge and wisdom. When we remember the stark truth that nothing is taught until something is learned, we grasp the secret of village sustainability. Villagers fully understood that survival was dependent on learning certain life skills basic to existence, and to learn those more and more effectively as each generation was trained to contribute to the ongoing life of the village. Those skills were learned and practiced. Hunting, clothing, agriculture, and a wealth of other daily life skills came as knowledge was transmitted from one generation to another.

Other life skills required the practicing of life together. These skills required both facts and their effective application for the creation of a social environment that was conducive to the easing and conquest of the tensions that come when people gather in any size group. To live together we must begin to catch on to how to interact, and as the old folks teach us, to learn from our mistakes. In this regard it is interesting to read of the critical importance of unstructured and structured play in the higher mammals and, of course, most vitally, in human development.

When I was growing up, our daily job as children was playing. The neighborhood kids would gather in the summer time to invent games, play group games, and sports. We would build tree houses, and always forts, and Christmas tree houses with discarded trees in the winter. We organized around all of these group activities with only a few basic tenets: You had to follow the rules (whatever they were), and cheaters were met with such disapproval that it always helped straighten them out. You had to stick up for the underdog, and therefore bullies were met with group solidarity that helped check their impulses. And you had to cooperate with the majority if you wanted to play. We didn't know it then, but this was good training for our life as adults.

It is precisely that kind of training and socialization that is missing in the lives of many young people today, especially in the neighborhoods where we intend to build Friendship Houses. The lack of safety, adequate dwellings, or healthcare, just to name a few, can compromise young people's ability to learn. Even in wealthier neighborhoods, where neighbors do not know one another, young people lack the kinds of opportunities for active play that so characterized the experiences of an earlier age. "Re-village-izing" our communities will mean among other things expanding the channels by which adults will pass on wisdom both formally and informally to young people and expanding opportunities for young people to be nourished by the socialization that play can provide.[7]

Leadership

Education, the acquisition and transmission of knowledge and wisdom from one generation to another, was a fundamental pillar

---

[7] The relationship between play and learning is well established. See, for example, Regina M. Milteer et al., "The Importance of Play in Promoting Healthy Child Development and Maintaining Strong Parent-Child Bond: Focus on Children in Poverty," *Pediatrics* 129, no. 1 (2012); Elena Bodrova and Deborah J. Leong, "The Importance of Play: Why Children Need to Play," *Early Childhood Today* 20, no. 1 (September 2005).

in the village structure. And the invention of the village was to improve that process exponentially. That is why leadership in the village was fundamental. The whole cooperative process had to be both directed and nurtured by some guiding means, which we understand as leadership. This fundamental element over the thousands of years of the village took many forms. The strong-man chief, the village council of elders, the collective voice of the villagers themselves, all had their day in the ebb and flow of the history of the village. Each had to have one overarching goal, and that was to make sure that the lives and life of the village itself were nourished by the most effective ways possible in order to both survive and thrive.

It was within the village that leadership became defined and perfected as an institutional fundamental. So much has been placed under the microscope of analysis about leadership that we are in danger of making it an abstract concept. There are wonderful books and seminars and even whole schools of leadership, but as we know, they all must lead themselves to the purpose of serving the community's basic purpose of providing the environment best for human life to thrive in every manner.

The servant-networker model of leadership that CRI is developing through our training equips men and women to build up the relational foundation of their villages. At every level—Renewal Team, Haven House, and Friendship House—leaders have the same mission: Community Renewal intentionally builds and grows positive, caring relationships. Leadership, in this context, is no longer abstract; it is about giving time and attention to the women, children, and men they see on a regular basis.

We have yet to discuss the eighth element of the village, the one that provides the very foundation for the other seven: mutually enhancing relationships. We turn to that element in the next chapter.

PART THREE

GROUNDING IN FRIENDSHIP

7

Mutually Enhancing Relationships

We have now discussed seven of the eight fundamentals of the village. It is strange, is it not, that we would go back to our societal roots to gain a glimpse of the road to hope for addressing our pressing challenge of creating a society that gets better both incrementally and generationally? But before we tell of the hope which the ever-renewing community brings (Chapter 8), let me share the last—and in my thinking, the first among equals—fundamental element composing the village structure. This element, mutually enhancing relationships, is not only fundamental—it is foundational. Every other element is in dynamic relationship with the village foundation because it springs from, flows into, and rests upon the very real relational connections of the villagers themselves. This indeed is the foundation just as surely as it is the wellspring of society. In order for society to function cooperatively, at the very base must be relationships that build one another up and strengthen one another in their interaction.

Relationships can be terribly destructive, and those kinds of relationships are omnipresent in every strata of societal development. We have all experienced our share of relationships that are not mutually enhancing. And when they are not, then they become fundamentally transactions that cannot ultimately be sustained, and therefore do not feed the life of the whole.

Early villagers knew that the entire village was dependent for its very survival on the way they were connected together in relationships that contributed to the well-being of each and of all. The ethic of the human relationships within the village was intentional, visible, and foundational to everything else that occurred. And unless this foundation was initiated, grown, and nourished quite intentionally with each generation, then the entire societal structure would collapse. But the very size of the village helped ensure that this relational foundation was front and center in seizing the conscious attention of the whole village itself. If there was trouble, everyone knew about it, and all worked together to make the disagreements right. The village depended on relationships.

It is obvious that the closer people are when they are connected in relationships that build one another up, then the stronger is the foundation upon which their society and culture rests. As I have said, one of the ineluctable rules of creating positive human relationships is the necessity of conscious intentionality. I can meet you by accident, but I cannot be your friend without intention. I must invest myself in our friendship, and I must refrain from those things that are destructive to our friendship. All of these things we know almost intuitively. And we learn by living how to become more and more skillful in their practice. So it is not difficult, when we take this truth as the very foundation and content of society itself, to answer Lewis Mumford's question regarding the mysteriously self-destructive nature of our societies: why do we continue to collapse the societies we construct? When we do not consciously and intentionally invest ourselves in relationships and give them attention, they diminish and will ultimately atrophy to the point of disintegration. Again, we know that from our personal experiences of friendship.

By close examination of the only human collectivity through the eons of the human race that has not collapsed since its invention, the village, we see clearly the necessity of that foundation. If we are to construct a house, the house must rest upon a firm foundation if it is to have a sustained presence. Then, the other fundamentals are built upon that foundation. We must have walls, a roof, and a door. Those are the fundamentals. Everything added beyond that is optional.

So, too, mutually enhancing relationships are fundamental to the basic house of society we call the village. They are the only fundamental element that is also foundational. And if the foundation disintegrates, then the house comes down. If the foundation is nonexistent, then constantly rebuilding the house is problematic at best. We understand this about houses, but how blurred our vision becomes when we dive into the realm of what appears to be the chaotic flux of society.

Think of it this way and the analogy gains some clarity: The foundation of every city and town rests upon a relational foundation. If that foundation collapses, then our city begins to disintegrate. This disintegration of our relational foundation then affects every other fundamental element of our society.

Let me bring this home. If your city disintegrates, then it is not good for your hospitals (healthcare), your schools (education), your economy (work), your safety (safety/security), your community (common values), your neighborhood housing (adequate dwelling), and your purposeful direction (leadership).

It is not a mystery why we keep collapsing the societies we construct. As we have grown away from the front-and-center attention that the village gave to the nurture of its living foundation, which was mutually enhancing relationships village wide, then we have experienced successive collapse. Disconnection brings dysfunction within human relationships. When we look closely and carefully using this relational prism as a means of examining the collapse of our societies, we see at its heart that it is a failure to intentionally, consciously, and effectively grow and nourish our relational foundation on a scale that is much more immense than that of the village. So we collapse.

The Missing Table

It is fascinating, historically, to see the reactions that societies began to have once the people truly sense that disintegration is happening. The vague feeling of discomfort begins to merge collectively into distress as the awareness dawns that things are not the same. I like to use the analogy of a table in a restaurant. When the table is present, you do not really notice it. Your attention is not riveted on its existence. To the contrary, you take for granted that its sturdy presence will be a place to rest your elbows, hold your place setting and your meal. You assume its presence. But suppose all at once, in a flash, after you and your party sat down to eat and were chatting away, the table disappeared. There would be a crash of all the plates, glasses, silverware, and in the South, ketchup bottles. And if you were leaning across the table to make a discussion point, you join the heap. What had no one's attention when it was present now has everyone's attention if it suddenly disappears.

So it is with the relational foundation of our society and cities. When it is present, we don't really notice it. We have made the critical error of "out of sight, out of mind" that every successive civilization has made growing away from the small village where human connectedness is very much in sight and in mind. When it begins to disappear, we don't notice anything but its progressive absence.

Unfortunately for our sake, this disintegration happens over the years with successive generations so slowly that it is almost imperceptible until the dysfunction of our relationships in our cities becomes so clear that all the king's horses and all the king's men can't put Humpty Dumpty together again.

I might say here that one of the causes of societal disintegration itself can be found in the fact that once we have laid down this dynamic and living foundation of mutually enhancing relationships upon which everything rests, it appears that we do, generationally and successively, grow away from the skills of our early builders. Each generation must be schooled in the absolute necessity and learned conscious skills of nourishing community. Otherwise it will begin to make the disastrous unconscious assumption that the relational foundation that made the community possible is altogether present, strong, vibrant, and eternal. And when we assume our relationships are so fine and so strong that we fail to give them intentional attention, or very nominal off-handed attention, then our relationships will disintegrate.

In like manner, upon initiating community, if we fail to give relationships front-row attention, we could never get off the ground. We all see that. But once joined, we must be cognizant that inattention at this stage is just as deadly a cancer as in the beginning of that relationship.

Each generation grows away from its wise builders and assumes that the table of the relational foundation for its community is eternal. If it was there when we got on board, we assume that it will be there when we depart. But without our investing time and attention, nothing could be further from the truth.

Furthermore, by inheriting a diminished form of societal organization, each generation loses not only the consciousness of the foundations and lifeblood of community, but it loses the ability and skills of growing and nourishing the essential element of human connectedness necessary for society to rest upon. The error of assuming is compounded by the ignorance of how to fix the problem.

We have come full circle. If Toynbee is correct in his definition of the very nature of society as a system of relationships, the enigma of repetitive societal collapse is resolved. For the answer is to always attend to the very foundation of all societies: our capacity to care for one another.

The Institutional Fallacy

Once we collectively perceive that our world is unraveling around us, our historical response is to try and repair the elements we can see, because we have become largely unconscious of the relational foundation that holds all things together in society. I call this the institutional fallacy. We are fully aware of our venerable institutions, which we inherited when we were born into human society. All of them, as we have seen, have grown out of their roots in the first societies we know as villages and have become ever more complex and sophisticated as they become cities. Our institutions—hospitals, schools, businesses, government, community organizations, faith groups, and all of the existing organizations serving the fundamental elements that have been described in the discussion of the village—are familiar to us. And as the vague awareness that something is beginning to rot in our midst turns into a conscious and omnipresent reality in our minds, we turn to the only thing that we know to stop the unraveling: our institutions.

We reason that if we can perfect the institutions that we believe are the heart and soul of society, then we will staunch the hemorrhaging of our security. So we march forward with picks and shovels to pour ourselves into constructing the bulwarks against the encroaching enemy of disintegration. Better businesses and education, more efficient government, relevant religion, innovative nonprofits, improved housing, more police, stronger military, and effective healthcare are all good things, but no matter how we try, we simply cannot touch the primary source of our coming apart.

For instance, I have heard so often that education is the answer. Well, honestly, it is not. Education is fundamental, but it is not foundational. It grew from and flows back to mutually enhancing relationships. And arguably, the most advanced nation in rigorous formal education in all of Europe disintegrated into a monstrously destructive force eating its own and then seeking to devour the whole of humankind. Germany went Nazi, and education did not stop the descent but accelerated it.

I have also heard the proposition that the answer to stop the slide has to be the creativity supplied by the entire individual entrepreneurial economic system. Again, I will surely grant that all meaningful work contributes to the good of the whole, but it is fundamental, not foundational. Rome had the greatest mercantile system ever seen in the history of the world in its day, but it was just like one of those magnificent elm trees where I come from. They are huge and beautiful but eventually all die from an inner rot. One cannot tell they are even sick until they suddenly land on your car.

No, the institutional fallacy evades a primary truth: there is no such thing as social osmosis. You can no more fix the foundations of a house by perfecting the door or walls or roof, than you can repair a disintegrating society by perfecting its institutions if you ignore the intentional repair of relational connectedness. No relationship can be healed through compensating for failing effectively and deliberately to invest oneself in that relationship, period.

The institutional fallacy at its heart is compensation. We are either unaware of the primary cause of our societal unraveling, or we are aware but unable to heal the problem. We then compensate by doing what we do know how to do based upon the institutional behavior handed down to us. Thus each society that begins the decline phase in effect begins madly to paint the deck chairs on the *Titanic*.

If your relationship is sick, it must be and can only be healed relationally. No diamond ring returns love to the throne. Unless, of course, it is undergirded and accompanied by all of the actions necessary to heal and recover a bruised or broken relationship. Our cities all rest upon a relational foundation. And this foundation, once it is laid, must be grown and nourished with skilled attention precisely because it is relational. There is no other answer.

Making Friendship Viral

Again, I must stress that all of the elements are fundamental to the village as well as to our society as a whole. All are therefore critically important in proving the setting for growing whole persons, but all rest on that one element that we have consistently taken as a matter of course, to our detriment. All of society is composed of, and rests upon, the relational foundation. I might add that many times in the presentation of this crucial reality, I have been greeted with an expert's yawn. As if to say, "Well of course that is always a part of the essential equation." Which is like saying, "Everyone knows that."

But the key truth lies in the understanding that relationships are utterly and completely foundational and therefore unless we know, fully know, how to initiate, grow, and nourish that organic and dynamic foundation both systematically and measurably, then we are whistling in the dark. I always ask these experts (and they truly are experts in their field), "Then tell me, how do you concretely start, grow, and nurture the relational foundation for whole cities, and for every city in the world, because that is the only way you will arrest the disintegration of our societies? Give me the steps of that process, how you will sustain it, and do you have a working model in place which effectively actualizes your concepts?" Normally I am greeted with totally blank stares. We have taken the critical element of our very corporate being and existence completely for granted with devastating consequence. Our human connectedness is not an addendum to civilization. It is civilization itself!

We have seen that we cannot attain the hope of a renewed and ever-renewing society without the rock-bottom reality that we must have better people if we are to have a better world. And we have also seen that the power to grow rests within the commitment to positive relationships, which then must be planted within a nurturing environment best suited for that growth to occur. Finally, we have shared that the ancient village structure became the culture within which the DNA of positive relationships could multiply exponentially. It is critical to understand exactly how the yeast that is the actual molecule of society (a positive relationship or friendship) can begin to permeate villages and then cities in order that they might be leavened entirely.

Remember the formula: to have a better world, you have to have better people. And to have better people, they must commit to enter and stay in positive relationships. Together, these positive relationships grow in the enlarged world of consciousness we call inclusiveness until every single human being is included. We generate renewed persons who are growing in wholeness within renewing friendships, and we replicate the conditions that make those relationships possible and sustainable by lifting up the primacy of positive relationships as the number one goal of life, knowing that everything must be subordinated as a means to this critical end.

I always share with people I meet, as we begin to discuss what community renewal is, that it is necessary to concentrate consciously on a new way of looking at things. We are all so intrigued by the massive forces around us and the headlines of everyday living that our attention is shifted quite subtly away from the absolutely vital. And so I illustrate the point by observing: "You and I just met. And we want to be friends. Now how in heaven's name can you and I getting to be friends begin to affect the massive dysfunction of the world around us? How can two people becoming friends stop the forces of destruction and evil and change everything? But stop and think. If indeed the very nature of this reality that we call human society really is a system of positive relationships, then the very molecules of which society consists are friendships. You and I are a molecule. We can be yeast for a whole new and ever-renewing society. The key is this: how do we begin to multiply this yeast so that friendship permeates the entire world?"

How in the world can you and I getting to be friends truly affect all of society? One of my favorite images—used by Jesus in all three Synoptic Gospels—is that of the mustard seed. It is a tiny seed, but once planted it becomes the largest of all of the plants in the garden, and the birds of the air all make their nests in its branches. You and I getting to be friends can change all of society if we can plant our friendship in the soil of civilization so as to reproduce the yeast of friendship in an exponential explosion. Or, in today's lingo, we have to find a way to make friendship viral!

8

The Ever-Renewing Community

In this chapter I want to share with you some of the ways we are growing an ever-renewing community through our efforts. These are recent stories—some are still in their early stages. But they all point to the ways that we are witness to a new model based on the primacy of intentional life together through connected caring relationships with one another. It is not only a theory—it is happening now.

I'll begin by pointing to a historical trend in the United States that highlights the need for this model, and then share seven stories that illustrate how the elements of the village structure (which I described in Chapter 6) are coming together in various ways, both in Shreveport and as far away as West Africa. The eighth element of mutually enhancing relationships, which I described in Chapter 7, pervades all of these stories, and in fact represents the ideal that evokes in people the desire to build and sustain the caring relationships which lead to an ever-renewing society. Committed caring together thus becomes the foundation as well as the living intrastructure of an ever-renewing community that will, like our loving friendships, only grow better and better, never to collapse.

A Historical Trend

We have learned how to build societies but not how to maintain them. What we can do with technology, we have yet to master for society. We can improve gadgets. It is an easy matter to discern the levels of development of cars or computers from one generation to the next. The computer that once filled a room can now be far outdistanced by the one that fits in your hand. The Model T is now the newest Tesla. The improvement in gadgets is both continuous and cumulative. But we have yet to find a way to build generations of humans into this "improvement" mode. We are caught on some ironic sorrow-go-round of a repetitive build/collapse cycle. You and I, unfortunately, are not new and improved versions of any of our civilized kindred who have gone long before.

By discerning challenges, both threatening and inspiring, both internal and external, and by banding together to successfully and successively meet those challenges, a disparate collection of individuals becomes molded into a dynamic collective of persons with one accord and one destiny. This is how societies are formed. Toynbee calls this process the "challenge/response" means of actually bringing people together to meet an external challenge or threat.[1] I call it the "provocative" means. It is when a perceived or real threat or challenge arises that we band together to meet it. It is like exercising a muscle with repetitions in the weight room. Muscle is built through continuous repetitions. So, too, societies in their solidarity through joining together in the challenge/response phenomenon. We are united in facing a challenge, but when the challenge or problem is met or solved, then little by little our unity dissolves.

---

[1] Arnold Toynbee, *A Study of History: Abridgement of Volumes I–VI*, ed. D. C. Somervell and David Churchill Somervell (New York: Oxford University Press, 1957), 81ff.

I believe that there is also an "evocative" means that can lead us toward lasting unity and an ever-renewing community. This unfolds when we experience a transcendent idea or ideal that evokes from us our lifelong devotion to its realization by means of our everyday choices. We can have individual devotion to everyday acts of caring for one another in friendship or marriage, and that devotion grows us better and better personally. So, too, can an entire society be devoted to the ideal of seeking the good of the other as we seek our own good, living that devotion on a daily basis through acts of caring for one another. Commitment to this pervasive ethic of caring on a daily basis can create an ever-renewing community.

Robert Putnam, that wise observer of American society, raised a caution flag when he published *Bowling Alone* at the turn of the millennium.[2] His thesis was that democracy itself, predicated as it is upon the free associations of individuals with one another for the sake of a common good, was imperiled by our slide toward individuality. More recently, in *The Upswing*, he focuses on our nation's progression from an "I" society in the Gilded Age to a "we" society that peaked in the 1960s, before collapsing once again in the past fifty years to become more individualistic.[3] In both books he maps our society's well-being with the story of much or how little we build bonds of caring for one another.

Our experience at CRI suggests that Putnam's thesis is correct. Relationships heal societies. I've already mentioned our successes: where a culture of caring is reestablished, communities

---

[2] Robert D. Putnam, *Bowling Alone: America's Declining Social Capital* (New York: Simon and Schuster, 2000).

[3] Robert D. Putnam, with Shaylyn Romney Garrett, *The Upswing: How America Came Together a Century Ago and How We Can Do It Again* (New York: Simon and Schuster, 2020): "The story of the American experiment in the twentieth century is one of a long upswing toward increasing solidarity, followed by a steep downturn into increasing individualism. From 'I' to 'we,' and back again to 'I'" (18).

thrive. Crime goes down. Homeownership and graduation rates increase. People open their doors and get to know their neighbors. Life is better.[4] It has already happened in Allendale. Next we will see it happen in the Martin Luther King neighborhood.

The Martin Luther King Jr. Neighborhood

In February 2022, I was thrilled to participate in a groundbreaking for our eleventh Friendship House in the Martin Luther King Jr. (MLK) neighborhood of Shreveport. CRI is partnering with Kansas City Southern Railroad (KCS), which owns the huge Deramus Train Yard located on the southern edge of MLK.

The partnership with KCS recalls in many ways the earliest days of launching Community Renewal. Pat Ottensmeyer, the president and CEO of KCS, speaks about why his company is investing in this neighborhood, using a logic that echoes what I heard from business leaders in Shreveport decades ago: thriving communities are good for business. "This is our home, too," Pat says to me, noting that over 630 KCS employees live and work in the area.

Pat understands that companies can be part of our Renewal Team and share the vision for a society as a system of mutually enhancing relationships. We spoke recently about how his company's mission aligns with our goals. It's not enough, he says, to set a low bar for a company mission, even something as basic as "we haul freight." For while that is certainly a main driver of the business, that goal won't easily inspire employees on the ground to do more than clock in and clock out. He points to the fact that purpose-driven corporations have an easier time attracting and retaining people, retaining customers, and promoting

---

[4] For a reflection on CRI's work, see Seth Kaplan, "Building Relationships, Strengthening Neighborhoods," *Stanford Social Innovation Review* (Fall 2021).

innovation.[5] The KCS mission, he says, is to make a "meaningful contribution to the economic growth and prosperity of the communities we serve."

Colin Mayer's and Bruno Roche's *Putting Purpose into Practice: The Economics of Mutuality* could be a playbook for the kind of thinking that KCS is showing in its multiyear commitment to the MLK neighborhood. Mayer, the founding dean and now Peter Moores Professor of Management Studies at the Saïd School of Business at the University of Oxford, and Roche, the former chief economist of Mars, Incorporated, argue that for too long the business world has been strangled by a narrow understanding of its purpose. Rooted in the work of Milton Friedman and the Chicago School of Business, this understanding limits business to the relentless pursuit of profit, an approach they describe as "progressively less efficient and effective and more destructive of value creation."[6] Successful organizations, they argue, are those which transcend self-interest and operate out of an economic model that stresses mutuality. Profit may be an indicator of good practice, but it is an insufficient measure of a company's success.

Like many companies during the pandemic, KCS saw the collapse of its business and the stress that it put on many of its workers and their families. That experience, Pat says, helped them to name how the railroad business is such an important part

---

[5] See BBC Capital, "Why Amazon, Facebook, and Airbnb placed Purpose First," www.bbc.com/storyworks/capital/the-purpose-driven-company/purpose-driven-companies; and the Harvard Business Review Analytics/EY Beacon Institute, "The Business Case for Purpose," hbr.org/resources/pdfs/comm/ey/19392HBRReportEY.pdf. Rebecca Henderson, the John and Natty McArthur University Professor at Harvard Business School, writes in the latter, "The sense of being part of something greater than yourself can lead to high levels of engagement, high levels of creativity, and the willingness to partner across functional and product boundaries within a company, which are hugely powerful."

[6] Colin Mayer and Bruno Roche, *Putting Purpose into Practice: The Economics of Mutuality* (New York: Oxford University Press, 2021), 3.

of the infrastructure of communities—both those that benefit from the movement of freight and those that supply the people who make the company work. The MLK neighborhood is one of those communities, and so partnering with CRI to build the foundation of that community was a natural choice.

At the groundbreaking, one of the KCS vice presidents, Carl Akins, spoke. Carl also happens to have grown up in the MLK neighborhood, and in his speech he recalled days of biking during the summer. Shreveport can get awfully hot in July and August, and so he and his friends would sometimes seek to escape the heat by going to the local branch of the public library. There, he would pick up books to read to escape boredom, and he gravitated toward books about engineering. Fast forward: Carl attended community college, then earned a bachelor's degree. After many years of working in science-related fields and earning two master's degrees, he returned home to Shreveport and began work for KCS. Carl was instrumental in helping us to partner with KCS to build the new Friendship House there, and we are excited to see the way this partnership will help us invest in that neighborhood.

In a remarkable turn of events, just a few months before the groundbreaking, Carl looked at the program for the event and learned that a childhood friend of his, Patrick Drew, had been named the community coordinator who would staff the new Friendship House. Patrick is a few years younger than Carl, but both remember each other from those early days in MLK. Patrick's story went a different direction from Carl's. Today, he describes a period in which everything he did was "tearing down the neighborhood," including selling drugs. He estimates that most of his friends from those days are serving life sentences in prison, and so he is profoundly grateful to have found the people who helped him ultimately make different choices.

Patrick met my dear friend Russell Minor, the director of our Haven House, who over time drew him into Community Renewal events. Something awakened in him when he contemplated the kids that he encountered in his neighborhood. He discerned that he could be a force for good in their lives, to help them avoid the choices that had gotten him into trouble and even sent him to jail for a stint. He began a ministry and called it Brothers Who Care, at first reaching two boys whom he saw breaking some glass outside his home. The CRI ethic of building and growing positive and caring relationships made immediate sense to him in that context: he could see that they were directionless, and that he could help steer them toward better choices than he had made at their age. Eventually he was leading a group of six boys, then fifteen, using his own money to mentor them. In his own mind he was using his ability to build up the neighborhood—a stark contrast to the tearing down he had fallen into in his youth. He became a Haven House leader, and before long we tapped him as the kind of person who could build on his desire to work with kids and named him the community coordinator of the new Friendship House in the MLK neighborhood. Patrick and his wife, Caronda, will continue ministering to the group of some forty kids that have gravitated to Patrick's work, and they will also enfold them into the Friendship House and its outreach to the families within a forty-block area. Having discovered the way that his experience of caring relationships was a source of renewal in his own life, he is bursting with excitement at evoking in others in the MLK neighborhood the desire to care.

Serving and Protecting

The groundbreaking for the MLK Friendship House was an event that the entire city of Shreveport could celebrate together.

One of the most visible elements of that celebration is itself a story of renewal that we are excited to see unfold. I am speaking of a police motorcade that accompanied our entourage from the CRI offices to the site of the new Friendship House on Legardy Street. This motorcade was not something that we sought out— rather, it was the Shreveport Police Department that reached out to us, wanting to be a visible part of this community-building event. The department invited its own officers to be part of a massive welcome to everyone participating in the event, lining the streets with celebratory signs.

We have been in partnership with the police from the begin- ning, realizing that we must have a safe environment in our city in order for people to feel secure enough to reach out and care for their neighbors. This is especially true in our highest-crime areas. As we built our Friendship Houses, our police gave us their increased presence for the first few years. That visible presence helped to create a safer neighborhood, enabling our community coordinators to grow the strongest caring relationships possible to begin the transformation of those areas from the inside out. In our partnership we have changed the concept of community policing to one of caring and policing, partnering to grow com- munity itself. So it was no accident that led to the wonderful intrinsic response of our friends in the department. They have provided the longitudinal study of over twenty years that points to how the five Friendship House neighborhoods show an aver- age reduction of crime of over 50 percent compared to the year before a Friendship House was established.[7]

---

[7] The Shreveport Police Department compiles data for several categories of crime in the five neighborhoods that have Friendship Houses, with the most recent report provided to CRI on November 10, 2021. Most notable is the comparison between rates of major crime the year before a Friendship House was established and the 2019 rates. Overall, there is a 55.75 percent drop in major crime during that period, and a 31.5 percent drop in total crime. Source: SPD Records Management System.

An example of our partnership is the annual National Night Out, which the Shreveport police hoped to use as an opportunity to be more visible in the community. Mindful of the tensions that have made relationships between police and communities of color difficult for decades, and never more so than in recent years, they met with us and the mayor's office to develop a strategy. Together, we aimed to double the number of block parties that were held across the city in Shreveport (this was before the pandemic). The stunning result of that effort was that *during that night, there were no reported crimes anywhere in the city.*

We met our target and more, hosting 170 block parties all around our city. For their part, the police put together care packages that they hand delivered to our hosts, spending time at each location to get to know neighbors. Their sole objective was to build positive relationships through caring. In some neighborhoods where residents recalled past tensions with police, either themselves or their friends and relatives in other cities, some expressed the desire that police not be present during the parties. Still, in one such case an officer arrived and with great sincerity communicated a simple desire to serve and to help out. It was a story of tensions diffused and the beginning of reconciliation.

The mayor's office, in turn, ensured that lack of resources in some neighborhoods was not an impediment to a block party. Seeing the vital opportunity to invite neighbors to get to know one another better, the mayor's office partnered with a local food bank and offered pickup stations at the Community Renewal main office. The police helped with the food distribution, and the parties went on! (Our Haven House leaders are fond of describing their work strategy: why have a meeting when you can have a party?)

This kind of partnership does not happen overnight. In fact, it is the fruit of many months of conversations spearheaded by one of the long-time staff at Community Renewal who happens to be my son, David. David had met for many months with a friend of CRI who had connections to both the mayor's office and the police. The man expressed how he was tired of hearing people gripe about problems in the city and so decided to do something. Realizing that it was critical to build a network, he turned to us.

Over time, this friend came to understand the way that CRI seeks to make a difference. He expressed to David how our approach has changed his life, challenging him to move beyond the pattern of transactional relationships that had characterized his personal and business life. Today, he has taken our tag line to heart: Community Renewal intentionally builds and grows positive, caring relationships. It permeates everything we do.

That same attitude is influencing the work of the police department; the police themselves are discerning ways that they might be part of building and growing positive and caring relationships throughout the city. They have seen up close that this model works. Allendale, to use one example, was once the most violent neighborhood, and now it is one of the safest.[8] Their work as police is not only easier, since it means keeping officers out of harm's way, but it is also more life-giving, both to them and to the people whom they serve. They are part of building a culture of safety and security that is integral to any village.

You may think that I have an unfulfilled longing to study Hymenoptera when I tell you that once again, recently, I was reminded of how ants can teach us something about how to build community. In this case it was the terrific story of some high schoolers and a slingshot. I am a fan of both. One of the former used the latter in fun, but errantly shot a clay ball into

---

[8] The SPD Records Management System report cited above indicates that in Allendale the number of total offenses reported has fallen by 61 percent between 2001 and 2019. The area that once had two homicides per week decades ago has reported no homicides for many years.

a Cecropia tree, creating an entry and exit wound. That was some shot.

Here is where it gets interesting. By the next morning, the Azteca ants that live in the tree had patched up the holes! The father of two of the boys is a scientist, and so he and the boys put together an experiment so they could understand what had happened. They observed that groups of ants would work together to patch the holes with plant fibers and sap, and many holes were completely patched within a day's time. The students partnered with a scientist and published their findings.[9] So consider the ants, and be wise! These creatures know (if we can say that) that a community must repair its home if it is to thrive. They must invest in care for the physical environment and work together to heal that which is in disrepair. The community must awaken to the reality that its future is in jeopardy if it fails to work in common toward shared ends. Remember the ants' formula: a simple act, put into a repetitive system, can solve a sophisticated challenge.

We have seen this in Allendale and in other neighborhoods around Shreveport-Bossier. People who work together to heal their physical environment benefit on multiple levels. I've focused on the way that our Friendship House neighborhoods show remarkable decreases in crime, but the story is much richer than that. Establishing a safe neighborhood, both by building foundations of connected caring and working with our local police, is just the beginning. We must also talk about the homes in which people make their lives.

Building Houses, Building Homes

We have shared that dwellings as well as safety and security are integral elements for the village. But what has become

---

[9] A. Wcislo et al., "Azteca Ants Repair Damage to Their Cecropia Host Plants," *Journal of Hymenoptera Research* 88 (2021): 61–70, doi.org/10.3897/jhr.88.75855.

abundantly clear over our past nearly three decades of work is that the rule of all real estate is also a rule that influences our relationships in society: it's all about location, location, location! For while it is true that our increasingly virtual world has made it possible to connect people across the world, still it is the people next door whom we see and with whom we interact, in either positive or negative ways. Whether we are talking massive houses in gated communities or next-door neighbors in an apartment complex, the physical location of our home matters.

That truth hit home to me in a new way in 2005 following Hurricane Katrina, which displaced many from their homes down south in New Orleans. Many of those people moved north to Shreveport, which saw a population bump of some twenty-five-thousand people. Knowing that this crisis would mean a desperate need for affordable housing, I sensed an opportunity for the residents of Allendale to remake their neighborhood. By then the Friendship House was in full swing, but around it were still dozens of decrepit shotgun houses barely fit for human habitation.

I went to visit my friend Millard Fuller and his wonderful wife, Linda, in Americus, Georgia. Millard and Linda had founded Habitat for Humanity years earlier, and by that point had built over 150,000 homes in ninety-two nations around the world. I had met him some fifteen years earlier, and we became friends. I knew that he could give our neighbors the opportunity to build better homes and make a significant change in the landscape of Allendale. They had the money and the resources to galvanize a community and offer residents the opportunity to obtain mortgages without interest. I invited him to come have a look.

Millard saw two things that persuaded him to work with us at Community Renewal. The first was that, at the time, the police told him they couldn't protect him if he went to work there. He took that as an invitation rather than a threat! That was Millard.

The other thing he saw was that Community Renewal was exactly what was needed for the community to thrive. Houses alone, he knew, couldn't do it. Good houses don't make good people! And there are too many scoundrels who live in mansions. No, what he knew was that houses are but one element in a thriving community, and that real transformation of a neighborhood takes place among people rather than buildings.

After a fallout with the national board leadership of Habitat, Millard established the Fuller Center for Housing in Americus in 2005. By October of that year it had partnered with us to launch the Building on Higher Ground initiative, building the first three of its houses around our Friendship House in Allendale. At the time we still called ourselves Shreveport-Bossier Community Renewal, but it was Millard who convinced us that we had to think about how our work might grow beyond our region. What good might come out of Shreveport-Bossier? (Millard had quipped, "I don't even know how to pronounce Bossier!") For that matter, what good might come out of a place like Americus, Georgia? Or Rochester, Minnesota? (That one's the Mayo Clinic.) So we rebranded ourselves Community Renewal International, as we were on the cusp of exporting our model to five villages in western Cameroon. Millard helped us to see that, like his work of building houses, our work of building communities could begin to remake the world.

Initially families were afraid to move into the new houses, fearing for their safety, but the Fuller Center people kept building. By the time they had built five or six houses, all of them around the Friendship House, they had reached a critical mass. Families moved in, knowing that their children could have a safe place at the Friendship House to play and participate in meaningful activities after school. Adults could access the Adult Renewal Academy to obtain a high school diploma if they needed to; network for job opportunities; learn a new skill; or simply meet their neighbors. Already the feel of the neighborhood was changing, and importantly, crime was decreasing.

For their part, the Fuller Center people considered this partnership a major win. They kept going, building upward of sixty houses throughout Allendale and in other parts of the city as well. They know that because of Community Renewal, the neighborhood will not be another slum in forty years. The homeowners are here to stay. They are committed to renewing their community because in many cases it is they themselves who put sweat equity into the construction of their houses in the first place, swinging hammers or hanging drywall. It is they who volunteer at Friendship House events, they who help coordinate activities for the neighborhood children, they who speak with their neighbors to build social capital. It is truly their neighborhood. "We Care" signs are everywhere. And with people like Pam Morgan—a woman who grew up on the streets of Allendale—staffing one of the Friendship Houses, the message to the residents is clear: this is our neighborhood, and we will ensure that it is a place where every child is loved and every resident is known and cared for.

We are now in conversation with the Fuller Center about undertaking a similar approach to one of the neighborhoods in Washington, DC, where plans are already under way to establish a Friendship House. My friend David Snell, who took over after Millard's passing in 2009, knows that it is possible to replicate what has happened in Allendale. We're excited to apply our social technology in our nation's capital, because we already have seen it work in places very different from Shreveport. Let me share two examples.

The International Houses of Friendship

My friend Valentin Miafo-Donfac first came to Community Renewal as an intern in 2006, while working on his graduate degree in nonprofit administration. A native of Cameroon, he was excited by the kind of renewal he saw happening throughout our city. He shared the story with the chief of his home village, and not long thereafter I was invited to share our story there.

It was my great honor to make a trip to Doumbouo, a group of five villages joined together in common cause. There I learned that I was to be designated an honorary chief, a brother to the five chiefs within the Bamileke tribe that had gathered to learn about Community Renewal International. During those ten days I shared with them our social technology and invited them to take the first step of making their caring for one another visible. The chiefs spoke of the very basic things they needed: access to clean water, electricity, a communication system, so many basic needs! At first they objected when I spoke about relationships. I had to persuade them that friendships can bring all these things in time, but first it was necessary to build a caring network, and thereafter to surface the resources that exist within that network.

Sometime after the trip Chief Fossokeng Solefack II Simon of the Batseng'la village began awarding "We Care" pins to the people who constituted the first Renewal Team there. They had to be nominated by two other people who testified to their acts of caring for others. The model of building connected, visible caring had begun.

Valentin understands the economic challenges in his country. Trained as a political scientist, he had been a professor at the University of Yaoundé. He sees young people leaving the subsistence-farming lifestyle to find education and jobs, often going to Yaoundé (the nation's capital) or even to other countries. The problems they are escaping are systemic: lack of infrastructure, lack of opportunity, lack of healthcare, lack of money, the list goes on. What attracted him to our model was our focus on restoring the caring foundation of society, a value consonant with what is at the heart of his tribal culture as well. He saw that CRI does not seek to impose a political or economic system, let alone export a particularly American way of doing things. On the contrary, what he sees is something much more fundamental to human experience that can be translated into a different culture without interrupting its most precious traditions.

I asked Valentin to join our staff to help us think about how we might replicate our model in places very different from Shreveport. Our experience in Cameroon helped us to think about that task. Once the chiefs began the process of developing a Renewal Team, the growth of a network of caring enabled them to begin planning an International House of Friendship. It is opening its doors in 2022, having been built entirely through funds they themselves have raised. Valentin describes it as a light in the local community, where people young and old will gather together, regardless of their backgrounds. Cameroon is a country of more than 240 tribes, and the language changes every seventy-five miles. Valentin understands the racial and cultural tensions that exist, but sees the International House of Friendship as a resource that will provide a bridge.

Recently, one of the women who has been involved in the Adult Renewal Academy, Hephzibah (Ene) Thomas, has begun replicating the CRI model in her hometown of Akpabuyo, Nigeria. Ene came to the United States a number of years ago, initially to do ministry and pursue education, and met James Thomas, a native of Allendale. It was James who initially had met people in CRI, but our Adult Renewal Academy coordinator, Gloria Millinder, recruited Ene to start a sewing class for some of the women in the program. From there, Ene came to understand our work and hatched a plan to replicate it in Nigeria. She saved some money and bought land in her hometown, launching another International House of Friendship that, while lacking the physical structure of a house, involves many of the kinds of programs that our Friendship Houses provide. They have begun to deploy the Haven House strategy among neighbors as well, building up the relational foundation of the village and committing themselves to the shared pursuit of sustainability.

Healthcare

Another exciting development that CRI is in the early stages of planning addresses the need in every village for a healthcare-delivery system. Since we have built and sustained relationships with people in high-need areas, we have known firsthand for many years that there are significant challenges that they can face in maintaining a healthy lifestyle. In 2003, the Robert Wood Johnson Foundation (RWJF) gave us a major grant to promote health in our community, knowing that we provided the relational network that could bridge healthcare/healthy lifestyle providers with at-risk communities. RWJF contracted with researchers who produced a report on how our model offered new possibilities for promoting public health.[10] They told me, "We know that good relationships bring good health, but we do not know how to form those relationships community-wide, and we believe that you have the model to make that breakthrough."

The research found that our model of building and growing positive, caring relationships affected the health of our communities in many measurable ways. For example, community coordinators might link a neighbor to a health-service provider and even offer a ride. They might offer opportunities for people to access mobile-health units at the Friendship House. They might offer events to promote health and encourage residents to quit

---

[10] Association for the Study and Development of Community, "Shreveport-Bossier Community Renewal: Background and Assessment of Evaluability and Recommendations," Robert Wood Johnson Foundation (September 16, 2003), section 2.4.

smoking or access routine preventative care. They might promote healthy eating by offering a cooking class or an afterschool program on healthy snacking. They might organize a neighborhood cleanup and promote a more hygienic environment. Perhaps most important, their presence in the neighborhood leads to less exposure to violence.

These are just a few of the snapshots that the researchers named as ways that CRI promotes public health. Our experience with the RWJF grant helped us to name things we were already doing and understand more about how our social technology addressed the health of neighbors in our Friendship House communities.

One of the major healthcare providers in Shreveport, CHRISTUS Health, took note of this role that CRI held and began offering small grants to support our efforts at promoting wellness. It actually provided a $250,000 grant that enabled us to hire community coordinators and initiate the entire Allendale Friendship House strategy. Over time, seeing the way that our focus on relationship building had far-reaching implications for promoting health, it invited us to apply for a large grant to support us in giving sustained attention to the social determinants of health. The US Department of Health and Human Services includes five major categories in these determinants: economic stability, education, healthcare access, neighborhood and built environment, and social and community context.[11] Because of our close association with people throughout the city, it perceived that we were in a position to help connect the people who could address all of these if they worked together.

---

[11] US Department of Health and Human Services, Office of Disease Prevention and Health Promotion, Healthy People 2030, "Social Determinants of Health," health.gov/healthypeople/objectives-and-data/social-determinants-health.

Judy Deshotels, a vice president at CHRISTUS Health, helped us to understand just how much we were already doing to address social determinants of health already. Whether addressing the mental health of neighborhood residents by building a caring network, or offering kids exercise and opportunities to develop friendships at our Friendship Houses, or helping neighbors to access fresh fruit and vegetables by planting a garden, CRI was, without knowing it, addressing all of them. For its part, CHRISTUS Health was happy to know that it had a community partner that shared the goal of promoting public health. We already had in place a structure that could be built upon.

Recently I learned of a study that showed how different countries dealt with the pandemic. Those that had high levels of trust—between citizens and in the government—fared best.[12] The article showed how trust is an important factor in public health and offered evidence of something that we have intuited for some time. It is that people's lives unfold within communities, and it is those communities that affect their decisions far more than any public service or advertising campaign. Our community coordinators do not work for an advertising firm, or a government, or even a hospital. They are members of the community. But they are also bridges to the rest of the city, meaning that they can both understand the health needs of our residents and point them toward the resources that they need in order to maintain or restore health. We are excited that they will be in a position to bridge people to the resources that CHRISTUS Health can provide as we continue to work together.

---

[12] Thomas J. Bollyky et al., "Pandemic Preparedness and COVID-19: An Exploratory Analysis of Infection and Fatality Rates, and Contextual Factors Associated with Preparedness in 177 Countries, from Jan 1, 2020, to Sept 30, 2021," *The Lancet*, February 1, 2022; https://doi.org/10.1016/S0140-6736(22)00172-6.

Education

That image of CRI being a bridge that connects people carries over into another story with tremendous promise. We are seeing the growth of a new model of our We Care Schools, made possible by one of volunteer Haven House leaders who connected us with Kasie Mainiero, the principal at University Elementary School in Shreveport, one of the most culturally diverse schools in the city. The school was in difficult shape when Kasie arrived, having been built for four hundred students and having then a population of three times that number! In a number of ways she inherited a system that was dysfunctional.

After several months of meetings with CRI, Kasie and her team engaged the entire school community, including parents, teachers, students, and partners, in an experiment to evoke responses to a shared desire: "We are creating pathways to a culture of caring as the foundation for learning and community. What will that look like?" The community generated a host of ideas and launched a Caught You Caring game in which all students could participate.

In the pilot year of the program (2018) the school handed out a number of awards to people who were "pathfinders," people with creativity and skill to develop and sustain new ways of caring for one another. One of the recipients was a fourth-grade student I'll call Victor, a socially awkward student who was not particularly good at relating to his classmates. He took it upon himself to watch out for unkind acts among other students at recess. He reported them to the assistant principal, Zachary Bolzan, who had been part of the We Care School pilot team.

Soon, Victor and Zachary were walking around at recess together. Zachary proposed to Victor that he become the recess patrol to encourage students in their acts of caring for one another. He donned an orange vest and carried a clipboard, inventing the new job as he went along. Victor's work soon attracted other students who wanted to help. He trained a second-in-command, and together they trained two dozen other students.

Initially, only teachers handed out Caught You Caring cards, awarding points to houses (in imitation of the house system in the *Harry Potter* series) when a student was caught caring for another student. Soon, however, Victor began handing out cards to both students and teachers. The idea caught on, and soon everyone wanted to be part of the effort of caring.

In that pilot year Zachary reported that behavioral and bullying reports at recess had ceased. At the nine-week assembly he asked how many of the fourth graders had worked for Victor. He estimates that two-thirds of the class cheered.

Victor's story is one of many that have emerged at University Elementary. The teachers report observations of positive change in the school. Many describe feeling greater care for one another, even across different grades. One teacher in particular, who was ready to retire because of frustrations with the education system, expressed great hope at what she saw happening at the school. Several observed the creative output that the Caught You Caring game had generated among students and teachers. Principal Kasie Mainiero observed that teachers were taking more time to get to know one another, and not falling into teacher cliques often seen in larger schools. Cafeteria and custodial staff showed a sense of being more valued and more a part of the school.

Among students, Kasie sees greater intentionality in caring. One notable example came from a substitute teacher who was encouraged to pursue full-time teaching because of a compliment from one of the students. In general, she sees better behavior across the school and rising levels of trust among students.

Kasie worked with Kim Mitchell, who oversees our Center for Community Renewal, to learn the model and train teachers and administrators. Kim is training leaders who are learning our methodology in order to establish it in other contexts, including both cities and schools. Kim has also worked with Tina Kendrick, a longtime educator who has relocated to Homer, Louisiana, to launch another We Care School there. Homer Elementary has similarly adopted the strategies of the Caught You Caring game and the house system and is already beginning to reap the results.

In addition to the elementary-school level, Community Renewal is happening in higher education. My *alma mater*, Texas Christian University, got on board in 2008 when I connected with my longtime friend Don Mills, the vice chancellor there. Knowing the kind of work we were doing, he brought a van full of student affairs professionals to Shreveport to learn more. Knowing then that a key concern in college housing offices was helping students to develop connections with other students and with faculty and staff, they adapted our three ingredients for a university setting. Don and Craig Allen, who oversees housing at the university, speak eloquently about the need for students to belong and to create and sustain positive, caring relationships. In particular, they point to the role of the resident assistant as parallel to that of the community coordinator at CRI; both are "natives" who live among the people they serve, connecting them to one another and to resources. Both approach their roles strategically, guided by an ethic of care. Both can exercise creativity and use their personal gifts and resources to reach their neighbors.

In this era when students at every level are showing high levels of stress, anxiety, and disconnection, I am hopeful that these models will grow and help our young people to thrive, even as they too learn to prioritize caring. The fundamental need in our communities is for leaders who care, who see in each person a precious gift. I've already mentioned that our Center for Community Renewal is training local leaders who are at various stages of building the CRI model from the ground up in a number of cities, towns, and villages. At this writing we are now in conversation with a college to develop a master's degree curriculum in community renewal, and we look forward to developing our growing network.

Calling Those Who Serve

It will be clear to all who read these pages that a key to building the ever-renewing community is the training of leaders capable of making visible the acts of caring that turn the tide of discontent in so many of our communities today. As I noted at the beginning of this chapter, what makes the emergence and sustaining of this kind of community possible is evoking in people the ideal of seeking the good of the other. Caring is natural, but it is not automatic. It must be evoked by people who have a fundamental understanding of the mission to serve.

For that reason, CRI is beginning an exciting effort to galvanize veterans of our armed forces to be part of our caring army. Like many of our staff and volunteers in Shreveport who are veterans, the men and women who have dedicated themselves to service already understand the principles necessary to carry out a mission. We are sounding the call to a new kind of service and will mobilize this army to begin their work in the towns and cities where they live. Recall the words of Dr. Martin Luther King Jr., who pointed out that those who love peace must organize as effectively as those who wage war.[13] We will reach out to veteran's organizations and work with community liaison officers to develop opportunities for those who are at the point of separation from active duty. Initially, we will ask them to be

---

[13] Martin Luther King Jr., "The Casualties of the War in Vietnam," address given at the Nation Institute, Los Angeles, California, January 25, 1967; published as a pamphlet by the Martin Luther King Jr. Center for Nonviolent Social Change, Atlanta, Georgia.

part of the We Care Team, to commit themselves to working with others in caring for the people in their neighborhoods. We will identify those who can take leadership roles as Haven House leaders, willing to connect people with one another and build lines of communication. And as we grow, we will assign those whom we've trained to be new community coordinators in Friendship Houses. Together, these people will work on a new mission: "re-village-izing" their towns and cities.

Conclusion

Remaking the World

In the early years of the twentieth century, one of America's most renowned philosophers, William James, was asked to deliver a lecture at Stanford University. James drank deeply of the history, the contemporary scene, and the future prospects of humankind living within communities throughout the world. It was in the title of this 1906 lecture that James coined his famous phrase "the moral equivalent of war!"[1]

I first read James's essay in April of 1981. I cannot tell you how deeply it burned itself into the fiber of my being. I pondered it wherever I went. Its truth made its way down the longest highway in the universe, it journeyed over the treacherous paths that led from my head down to the deepest part of my heart. That eighteen inches from the top of our brains to the bottom of our hearts means the difference between reading a statement and letting a truth read you! It has now fully seized my life, and I live to fulfill its promise.

Like James, I think of war. I have studied wars and their strategies from Peloponnesian to Punic up through modern times. I have read countless books on military strategy and the generals and nobles who propagated each plan. Like James, I have seen

---

[1] William James, "The Moral Equivalent of War," 1910 essay based on a speech at Stanford University in 1906, https://www.uky.edu/~eushe2/Pajares/moral.html.

how war can totally mobilize the intelligence, the industry, and the resources of a society to achieve one goal—victory. As James points out, in preparing for war and in waging that war, hearts are set ablaze and everything becomes subordinate to the goal. War becomes the unifying matrix of all of our energies and inventions, and we wage it ferociously. And those are the characteristics we must bring to our battle for the heart of our society. To understand what James is saying, I think of war.

Speaking from my years of experience, I would state James's insight this way: *if we are to renew society, if we are to remake the world, we must wage the moral equivalent of war.* And there is something more important to think about. How can we ever transcend the destructive wreckage of war? We must copy all that war does to energize and mobilize for use on a higher plane. It is the mobilization of all of our resources. It is the willingness to sacrifice all of our lives. It is the inspiration of all of our best thinking to marshal our collective energy to see that our children and their children can inherit a world of joy, peace, caring, and love.

Today, here where Community Renewal is working, I see thousands rallying to that hope for a better future. I see the moral equivalent of war beginning to grasp us and use us in effective ways. I was reminded of this image when Jerome Cox, a prominent Haven House leader, gave a keynote address at our Adult Renewal Academy banquet not long ago. When he was younger, Jerome fought with the Army Airborne Rangers, and later he returned home to become the CEO and founder of St. Mark Hospice. Jerome reminded us of a phrase from the Ranger Creed: "I will never leave a fallen comrade to fall into the hands of the enemy."[2]

---

[2] For the full text of the creed, see US Army, "Ranger Creed," http://www.army.mil/values/ranger.html.

Yes! That faceless enemy is here and everywhere. And so, against this ruthless enemy that destroys hope and takes the sparkle from the eyes of children, against this heartless enemy that blows up families and steals minds with opiates, against this soulless enemy that spoils future generations by ravaging neighborhoods, we must ever resolve to join an army of caring human beings who will march off to a new kind of warfare and never leave our wounded to fall into the hands of the enemy.

How shall we respond? As I ponder this question, I call to mind another question asked by the Reverend Sam Shoemaker in his last sermon before retirement from his pulpit at Calvary Episcopal Church in Pittsburgh: "Can our kind of church change our kind of world?" Think of it! Walk that question into the variegated institutions of our society and let it begin its pruning and shaping work. Can our kind of business change our kind of world? Can our kind of school change our kind of world? Can our kind of city change our kind of world?

Shoemaker's question has dogged my steps, and it will not let me rest. It points to the salient fact that we are here on Planet Earth to do something of significance beyond ourselves. I believe that we are called to remake the world. We are called to be "instruments of peace," as St. Francis of Assisi put it. We are to be partners in the grand construction of a globe filled with loving human beings dedicated to the preciousness of every single person. I believe that everything we do must have this point and this plumb line in place to give us our compass for the journey of life: are we seeking and serving for a new world to be born or are we seeking to be served? Ask the question! Things will begin to happen.

I believe that William James would have recognized that if our kind of movement is going to have a chance at changing the world, then we must be actively mobilized, efficiently trained, adequately armed, effectively supported, strategically utilized, and willingly sacrificed. Only then do we have a chance to meet the great test for which we were all born: to live lives saturated with meaning, because we live for one another.

Unfortunately, we have dithered. We have contented ourselves with being an audience rather than becoming an army. This is nothing new. In every generation people have more or less bought into the same subtle drift of thinking that as long as they join an audience—whether a congregation, a political party, or even a movement—they are doing something useful. An audience, however, is not worth working for. An audience is a set of unrelated people drawn together by short-lived attraction, a number of human filings drawn into position by a magnetic speaker. It will drop away as soon as the magnet is removed.

How do we move from being just an audience to becoming a forceful army for the building of a new world? The primary reality of our lives must first be recognized unashamedly. And that primary reality is just this: we can't do it. We are weak, idiotic, blind, and full of a whole menagerie of conflicting urges. As C. S. Lewis said about himself: "For the first time I examined myself with a seriously practical purpose. And there I found what appalled me; a zoo of lusts, a bedlam of ambitions, a nursery of fears, a harem of fondled hatreds."[3] But with that honest recognition, transformation begins.

The profound truth, repeated innumerable times throughout history, is that the world has been changed by broken people who were poor in spirit, but who joined with others and became an army. We are in a real war, and in order to win, we must meet and fulfill the conditions and principles necessary to win:

- We must have a clear understanding of what victory means.
- We must articulate a contagious understanding of victory.

---

[3] C. S. Lewis, *Surprised by Joy: The Shape of My Early Life* (New York: Harcourt, Brace and World), 226.

- We must have leadership that understands victory and knows how to achieve it.
- We must have a simple strategy to achieve that victory.
- We must have definable steps to take to follow the strategy.
- We must be trained and equipped to take those steps.
- We must be committed to sacrifice everything, even our lives, to win.
- We must be armed with adequate weaponry with which to fight.
- We must have the unqualified and sacrificial support of the home front.

Our struggle is not against any group of people. It is not against any one person. It is against the forces that make us less than our best, most generous selves. It is against conditions that destroy people and the unseen powers that in some inexplicable way pit us against one another and then discard us after we are empty.

At CRI we are working to define, measure, and fulfill each principle to win this war for the heart and soul of our cities and our societies. And please remember that we do not intend to preserve the present state of things. That would mean true defeat. Victory can only mean the radical transformation of our lives and our communities from pervasive self-centeredness to caring, other-centered living. We need everyone to join in this mighty effort as we unite across racial, denominational, and social lines to fight the good fight and to win victory.

We are building a movement of caring that stretches across the country and even around the world. We intend to awaken in people that which is most natural: the power to care. And in order to join our army, you need only be a human being.

Our intention is to remake the world. Already, we are seeing the fruits of our efforts, verified by researchers, civic leaders, police forces, and residents in the neighborhoods where our model has taken root and grown. Quite simply, our plan is that what we see in places where the CRI model is taking root will happen everywhere. We are building a culture of caring, and little by little removing the barriers that keep us from thriving. We are seeing the birth of hope in places where once there was none.

Let us join together in common caring to remake the world. Please visit communityrenewal.us to join us.

Afterword

by Anne Snyder

How well I remember the instant rearranging of socio-emotional chemicals upon arriving in Shreveport for the first time. It was late January 2017, and I was moving back to Washington, DC, from Houston, where a life shattered by loss had been knit back together by a patchwork quilt of institutions that understood the power of positive relationships to hold and to heal. Still, nothing could have prepared me for the contagion of care awaiting me as I pulled up to the offices of Community Renewal in a dusty red hatchback.

A tall, elderly southern gentleman leapt out of one of the organization's jeeps, bounding forward with a gait that struck me as a cross between a cowboy and a scholar. Mack McCarter gave me a hearty handshake and then, with enthusiastic southern charm, ushered me inside, where a circle of warm faces awaited my welcome for the weekly Quaker meditation. "When we gather here," Mack said softly, "we pledge neither to speak nor to remain silent. We wait for God to draw through us what he will."

It was an introduction to a communal dance at its most discerning. These staff members were the generals of a burgeoning army of community shepherds, some of them Haven House leaders, some of them residential stewards of one of the Friend-ship Houses, some of them serving as the administrative mortar holding it all together. They aired testimonies of praise from the last week of daily neighboring, the blend of trust in one another while honoring the confidences of those within their care at once deft yet self-disciplined. And they welcomed me with the sort of joy that makes you feel like *you* are the gift, though you've done nothing but show up. I felt every personal insecurity and wound melt away. "Here was perfect love," I thought. Here was the logic of John's epistles bearing out—a perfect love could indeed cast out fear.

It has been over five years since this induction into a different way of life, and while the magic of Community Renewal *does* reside in the people I met that first day, I've come to see that the real generativity is in the *science of human relations* that Mack and his team have uncovered and figured out how to model across a modern city. This is no naive group. Community Renewal understands that we live in a fallen world, fractured by injustice and human selfishness, generational sin, and corrupt powers. And yet, the group doesn't give up on our human capacity to care—every single one of us. Its job is to sow the conditions in a place such that each one of our gifts and wounds might find its electrical outlet to initiate, create, and sustain the life that is really life: communion with one another, the beloved community. These are conditions that can be named. They can be replicated anywhere.

When Martin Luther King Jr. was asked to reflect on the philosophical journey that led him to nonviolence as the only method truly able to resist social evil, he recalled a time when he had been reading Nietzsche's *Will to Power* and *The Genealogy of Morals*.

During this period I had about despaired of the power of love in solving social problems. . . . Nietzsche's glorification of power—in his theory all life expressed the will to power—was an outgrowth of his contempt for ordinary morals. He attacked the whole of the Hebraic-Christian morality—with its virtues of piety and humility, its other-worldliness and its attitude toward suffering—as the glorification of weakness, as making virtues out of necessity and impotence. He looked to the development of a superman who would surpass man as man surpassed the ape.[1]

(Mack McCarter could probably say something very similar in his long road to understanding the shape of kingdom possibilities in the here and now.)

But then Dr. King learned of Mahatma Gandhi, and he watched a peaceful miracle from the streets captivate the world. Dr. King adapted Gandhi's methods to Selma, and then to Montgomery. "Living through the actual experience of the protest," King wrote with gratitude, "nonviolence became more than a method to which I gave intellectual assent; it became a commitment to a way of life. Many issues I had not cleared up intellectually concerning nonviolence were now solved in the sphere of practical action."[2]

This is the task before you now, before me: to throw your life upon the principles Mack has elucidated with such heart here and to be surprised by joy. As he said to me recently, with tears, "Anne, daggum it, I'm just so glad I didn't miss the kingdom. I could have so easily missed it."

May this book be the grace that keeps each one of us from missing it too.

---

[1] Martin Luther King Jr., "Pilgrimage to Nonviolence," in *Stride toward Freedom: The Montgomery Story* (New York: Harper and Row, 1958), 95–96.

[2] King.

Acknowledgments

All of us should undertake to write a page of acknowledgments while on this side of the great mysterious divide to which we are tending. This is my first time to look back and capture on paper the multitude of folks who formed me and who sustain me still. I feel an utter eruption of gratitude, one I cannot help but also wish for you. So when you place on parchment your own celebration of those who helped you learn to walk, walked with you, and taught you where to walk, you will feel what I am feeling now. And it is simply wonderful because it is pure community. On my knees with my head bowed and with my eyes closed so that I may behold the faces of a multitude, I say from the core of all that I am and still hope to be, thank you.

To Judy, my soulmate, our children, their spouses, and our grands: you are always and forever.

To my family: my mom and dad and sister; grandparents, aunts, uncles, and cousins aplenty.

To my friends spanning a lifetime of love and laughter dotted with tears of seventy-five years.

To my teachers: I honestly see all of your faces and still feel your molding hands.

To the family of faith of the Kings Highway Christian Church who birthed me and grew me.

To the congregations of the three First Christian Churches whose love matured us.

To the members of the Mount Canaan Missionary Baptist Church who gave us a home.

To the Catholic Diocese of Shreveport and its congregants who have so richly enfolded us.

To the seers, thinkers, proclaimers, and doers upon whose shoulders we all stand and reach.

And to the team of Community Renewal International: Our truly sacrificially dedicated staff, past and present; our board members both functional and advisory; our We Care Team members everywhere. History will tell your story with trumpets and cheers because you blazed a trail that became a path and then a road and finally a highway. You led the way to a new tomorrow for all of humanity to follow to the world where Love will reign in each for each and all.

All of such produce a book.

The Introduction was first published as "I Saw a Man Fly! I Am Sure I Did!" in *Comment*, a publication of Cardus, on February 20, 2020. Part of Chapter 1, on David Elton Trueblood, appeared in the article "A Society of Friends" in *Comment*, a publication of Cardus, on December 1, 2017. Thank you to *Comment* for permission to reprint from those pieces.